MW00717231

You Can't
Be Serious

ALSO BY RALPH SCHOENSTEIN:

The Block
Time Lurches On
With T-Shirts & Beer Mugs for All
I Hear America Mating
Wasted on the Young
Yes, My Darling Daughters
Citizen Paul
The I-Hate-Preppies Handbook
Alma Matters
Every Day Is Sunday
Diamonds for Lori and Me

WITH BILL COSBY:

Fatherhood
Time Flies
Love and Marriage

YOU CAN'T BE SERIOUS

WRITING AND LIVING AMERICAN HUMOR

~

Ralph Schoenstein

ST. MARTIN'S PRESS   NEW YORK

YOU CAN'T BE SERIOUS. Copyright © 1990 by Ralph Schoenstein. All rights reserved. Printed in the United States of America. No part of this book may be used or reproduced in any manner whatsoever without written permission except in the case of brief quotations embodied in critical articles or reviews. For informaiton, address St. Martin's Press, 175 Fifth Avenue, New York, N.Y. 10010.

Library of Congress Cataloging-in-Publication Data

Schoenstein, Ralph, 1933-
    You can't be serious / by Ralph Schoenstein.
        p.   cm.
    ISBN 0-312-05190-5
        1. Schoenstein, Ralph, 1933- . 2. Humorists, American—20th century—Biography.   3. Journalists—United States—Biography.
    4. Authors, American—20th century—Biography.   I. Title.
PN2287.S336A3   1990
818'.5409—dc20
[B]   90-37234
                                                                          CIP

First Edition: December 1990

10   9   8   7   6   5   4   3   2   1

Born with the gift of laughter and the
sense that the world was mad.
—RAFAEL SABATINI

Dem is da conditions dat prevail.
—JAMES DURANTE

For Judy, Jill, Eve-Lynn, Lori, and Loren
The part that isn't absurd

For their wisdom and encouragement during the writing of a dangerous book, I am indebted to three classy men of letters and three treasured friends (which does not mean six):

Tom McCormack, editor nonpareil, who found me two steps in the hundred.
Norman Corwin, poet of the airwaves and sage of the page.
Bill Heinz, one of the great voices of American sport.

1

~

A Side Order of Prose

In the beginning, because I was ignorant, I wanted to be a lawyer. Instinctively, I must have known that America was a nation of suers and the suer system was run by lawyers. My grandfather, however, had a higher legal dream for me.

"With a mouth like yours," he used to tell me, "you could be another Dewey."

He didn't mean Donald Duck's nephew but Thomas E. Dewey, the great Manhattan district attorney.

"Ralphie, you can make it," he said one day. "They let Jews be DAs."

"And singers too," I told him. "Gramp, here's a big one I just heard from one of Pop's reporters: Dinah *Shore* is Jewish."

He smiled incredulously. "Dinah *Shore?* The *blonde* one with the Southern accent? She's one of *my* kind?"

By "my kind," he didn't mean an unemployed florist: he meant a Jew like him and like the boy who would be as famous as Dinah Shore when I became Mister District Attorney and

3

ended crime in New York. But my grandfather never knew that I had a secret dream: to conduct an orchestra. Night after night, I would put on the most stirring passages of immortal music, and conduct with all the style of a nurse shaking down a thermometer. Perhaps I could be a district attorney who conducted on the side: spending the day getting people to sing and doing the same thing at night.

And then, when I was twelve, I started high school and fell in love with the English language. Nineteen forty-five was one of the last good years for the English language: it was still being spoken in public schools. Nineteen forty-five was a time before children had begun reversing evolution by saying, "Hopefully, him and me will be like having a fun time" and other sounds from before the dawn of civilization. By performing in the winged radio plays of Norman Corwin, I suddenly saw that language could be used for something more exalted than saying "Up yours with gauze," a popular prescription on my block.

By the time I went off to Hamilton College, I was writing radio plays of my own, some of them versions of a weekly historical drama called *CBS Is There*. One of my plays, *CBS Is There at the Birth of Jesus*, contained this deathless exchange:

> FIRST WISE MAN: Look! In the barn! A baby in a manager!
>
> SECOND WISE MAN: What a miracle has come to the manager!

I was already learning about the liberties that art could take with life, especially in the mind of a Jewish boy whose strength was not describing barns.

What *was* my strength? I now was writing radio plays—some derivative and some uniquely rotten—and also short trite pieces about the greatness of Ted Williams and DiMaggio and Clipper, my cocker spaniel who had died from eating roach poison, a piece so overwrought that it would have made most readers root for the exterminator. My strength was not sporting nor canine cliché; and neither was it historical drama, for I managed to make Eleanor Roosevelt and Gandhi sound alike, and not too different from Aaron Burr. I had learned in freshman English that all of George Bernard Shaw's characters were really Shaw. Were all of mine really *me*? If so, who *was* I and was I worth listening to?

I surely was not worth hearing in a short story called "Sholom," in which an Israeli girl, Hilde Helfman, and a Jordanian boy, Abdul Ben Mohammed, transcended the hatred of their people to become two characters a reader could hate. With a feel for the Middle East that came from knowing Amsterdam Avenue, I borrowed from both *Romeo and Juliet* and *Dick and Jane Go to Palestine* to write such memorable passages as:

> "Where do you live, Hilde?"
> Hilde pointed back across the desert. "Over there—on a farm in Beersheeba."
> "Beersheeba!" exclaimed Benny. "But that's across the border in Israel! What in the name of Mohammed are you doing over here in Jordan?"
> Hilde gasped. "Oh, this is awful. I was chasing a butterfly and must have crossed over by mistake. I was looking in the air all the time."
> "Suffering sultans! You are lucky the border guards do not shoot you!"
> "Oh, this is terrible, Benny. I must hurry home if I ever wish to see another Sabbath."

It was the kind of dialogue that would have made a reader take delight in a holy war.

Not only was I trite in the Middle East, but I also had a flair for native American cliché that was far ahead of its time. This opening from a radio play that I wrote at fourteen reveals a command of the style that dominates televised sports today:

> NARRATOR: It's 1936. Football is sweeping the country like a house on fire. New stars are being born. Any tall lad

with a tough hide, a burst of speed, and a love for the game would surely make good. Ours is the story of such a lad. A big, speedy, freckle-faced lad from Oklahoma, who climbed into football immortality and into the heart of every fan. But we'll start from the beginning—in 1936.

In 1947, the essence of my creative gift was a talent for keeping track of the year—and, of course, the talent to inspire a freckle-faced lad to achieve the gymnastic genius of climbing into both immortality and the heart of every fan.

Three years later, when I was a sophomore at Hamilton College, my favorite reading had become James Thurber's hilarious stories about his early life, like "University Days," in which he told of a football player named Bolenciecwcz, "not dumber than an ox but not any smarter," being asked by an economics professor to name three means of transportation:

"Ding, dong, ding, dong," he said hopefully. Bolenciecwcz was staring at the floor now, trying to think, his great brow furrowed, his huge hands rubbing together, his face red.
"How did you come to college this year, Mr. Bolenciecwcz?" asked the professor. "*Chuffa* chuffa, *chuffa* chuffa."
"M' father sent me," said the football player.
"What *on*?" asked the professor.
"I git an 'lowance."

It was while reading this particular story that I felt it happen: a wonderful moment of truth in which I suddenly said to myself, as the dancer in A *Chorus Line* would say many years later, *I can do that!* Here was a bolt of lightning illuminating my own voice.

At once, working with more command and focus than I had ever known, I wrote a comic essay about the Hamilton genetics class in which I was haplessly fulfilling the college's science requirement by breeding fruit flies to study their genes.

To examine a fruit fly on the slide of a microscope, you had to anesthetize it with just the right amount of chloroform or turpentine or something else that I cannot remember because science itself has always anesthetized *me.* Too much chloroform and your fly was lunch for a frog; too little and he awoke on the slide and rose singing "Born Free."

In spite of my being as befogged as the flies, I did not mind supervising their sex because they bred in banana media and I loved bananas; in fact, my favorite food was banana cream pie, hold the flies. However, even my passion for eating their motel could not prevent me from losing track of the generations, for not only does no fruit fly ever look its age, but fruit flies mock birth control by reproducing every two or three days; and the children, biblical in range, so strongly resemble everyone else that they can be distinguished only by another fly or by a student whose grasp of genetics goes beyond mashing bananas. My flies were a definitively extended family in which I found myself trying to track the genes that offspring had given their parents.

While writing this story, I knew that I had left Hilde's desert for fertile ground: as a biological bumbler, I stood shakily with Thurber, whose biology professor, after looking at one of Thurber's renderings of what he had seen through his microscope, told him, "You've drawn your *eye.*"

When I had finished "No Flies on Me," I showed it to Professor Thomas McNaughton Johnston, who had been enriching my appreciation of the glory possible in English prose. Years later, had he not already been dead, "impact" becoming a verb would have killed him.

"This story is excellent," he told me. "Nothing is harder to sustain than humor and you seem to have the touch."

I wanted to embrace him and tell him that I would fight for his tenure. And what did he mean by "*seem* to"?

"It just felt natural to me," I said, giving him a chance to offer more praise.

"Oh, it has lapses, of course." I should have quit with sustaining the touch. "Be careful of elegant variation: don't be afraid to repeat a word, if that's the word you want again. And there's circumlocution on page three: say a thing directly, not roundabout. But you've found a language, Ralph, to match your tilted view of the world. Forget Warren Harding and do more about yourself."

Elated by Johnston's response to "No Flies on Me," and thinking of Thurber's stories about his dotty grandfather, I now wrote a story about helping my grandfather build his collection of famous Jews.

"*Gramp, here's a* beauty!" I said in "The Scorekeeper of Zion." "*The American Revolution was financed by a guy whose first name was* Israel!"

"*No good, Ralphie,*" he replied. "*We've already got too many money men.*"

"*So what are we short on?*"

"*Center fielders, princes, and Secretaries of State.*"

One day near the end of my junior year, I told him and my father that I couldn't be a lawyer because I was going to be a writer. Both of these men had suffered financially in the Great Depression, which seemed like a boom compared to their depression on hearing that I wanted to write stories instead of briefs. In panic, my grandfather gave me examples of celebrated writers who spent most of their time doing something legitimate and wrote on the side: Matthew Arnold, A. J. Cronin, Wallace Stevens, Howard Dietz, and Arthur Conan Doyle. He left out Adolf Hitler.

"You *have* to get a weekly check," said my father, "and a welfare check doesn't count. Writing is just too risky."

"But *Pop*," I said incredulously to the City Editor of the *New York Journal-American*, "your paper is *full* of writers."

"They're not writers, they're reporters. They're on staff and half of 'em can't spell. The other half are reformed drunks, and it was probably writing that drove 'em to it."

All these words of alarm, however, had been spoken in vain,

for the obsession to write already had taken possession of me. I was writing constantly, for life did not seem valid until I had put it on a page, reshaping it into a blend of fact and fancy. I was waking up at night to make notes that I often understood in the morning, sentences for stories that kept coming to me when I was supposed to be thinking about the Treaty of Paris or passing the salt; and I was feeling that every conversation was just a bad first draft and the talkers should have been using scripts, the kind of feeling that can lead a writer to a quiet den at the Menninger Clinic. Endlessly distracted by what was cooking in my little absent mind, I now understood James Thurber's saying that he had lost track of what had really happened to him and what he had made up, a twilight world where I felt I belonged because life was never coherent or entertaining enough for me.

In describing my work with cheerful pomposity, I once told a history teacher, "You see, as a writer, I'm making order out of chaos."

"My, my," he replied. "You sound like God."

I did feel godlike, however, in mixing the truth with what should have happened. This particular talent was a legal one too, but a writer's lies now seemed far better than a lawyer's to me. Moreover, my family knew many lawyers and I felt there was no need for another. What I didn't know, of course, in those early innocent years, was that America had even more writers than lawyers. Most Americans hadn't passed the bar, but *everyone* knew the alphabet and people disguised as doormen, beauticians, and CPAs were saying, "There's a fantastic book in me and I definitely could write it if I only knew what words came next."

But something, perhaps traumatic toilet training or too many early baths with my sister, was sending the words to me. In my senior year at Columbia College, where I had transferred to study English with men like Mark Van Doren and Joseph Wood Krutch, I won first prize in a WKCR radio writing contest: fifty dollars worth of records from Sam Goody's. My work seemed to be maturing: instead of a play like my one about the building of the Panama Canal, in which Teddy Roosevelt had said, "The fever may be yellow, but our hearts are red, white, and blue," I had written a play about a race riot in Cicero, Illinois, and I had even waxed creative with the name of the governor, "Addie Stevenson." Although violating Professor Johnston's suggestion to write about myself with humor, I had made the script work in its own solemn way by staying beneath the security blanket of *CBS Is There*, instead of having the courage to do something like a script about the days at Hamilton when I was biologically bananas.

Although my Columbia triumph left my father with both pride in me and also fear that I was merrily sailing away from a living wage, those records from Goody's made me giddy with delight, for I had won them with my writing. And when I brought them home, I gave vent to the greatest exhilaration I had ever known by going into my bedroom, closing the door, and conducting Beethoven's Fifth Symphony like a man fighting off bees.

Ten weeks later, the United States Army, aware that the war in Korea already had been lost, gave me my first opportunity to receive a weekly check. On the morning that I left for the Army Induction Station at the lower tip of Manhattan, my grandfather came to me and said with all his heart, "If you were in law school, you wouldn't be going. The Chinese haven't shot one lawyer."

And then I was off to Fort Dix, carrying a small flight bag that contained boxer shorts, Salinger's stories, pajamas, Hershey bars, and a composition book in which I was constantly putting down notes about moments in my life so that they would be real. At the age of twenty, I was already possessed by the feeling that events were made legitimate only by my pen. At the age of twenty, I was already mad, seemingly a prerequisite for writing well: I had just read Max Beerbohm's words: *I have known no man of genius who had not to pay, in some defect either psychical or spiritual, for what the gods had given him.*

Anxious to know what kind of talent the gods had given me,

at Fort Dix I moved up from random notes to a supposedly comic diary of the memorable moments in my basic training, one of which involved the diary itself. On a cold October morning at the Ninth Division rifle range, I had just put down my M-1 to make an entry in the notebook I always carried, sometimes in place of my field pack:

> There are guys in this company who couldn't commit suicide with an M-1. Our next war better be with pacifists.

Suddenly, from above me, I heard the charmless Southern drawl of my First Sergeant:

"Young trooper, what the hell are you writin'?"

"Oh—nothing, Sergeant," I said, giving my work a fitting critique.

"You know what your *enemy* is writin'? He's writin', *I gotta remember how easy it's gonna be to kill that jackass with the notebook.* Tell me, young trooper, you one o' them goddam *English* majors?"

"Well, I actually had a double—"

"'Cause the enemy's *got* no English majors. Just Chinese majors who are gonna blow off your ass."

And there, in dirt and disgrace, with visions of my disassembled ass dancing in my head, I couldn't wait for the sergeant to walk away so I could pick up not my rifle but the other weapon I had chosen for coping with life: my semiautomatic Scripto. As I wrote down what the sergeant had said, and also what he could have said, I somehow sensed that it was irrelevant whether I *wanted* to become a writer or a lawyer or a singing podiatrist: I *was* a writer, a mental unbalance that would always be as fundamental a part of my makeup—and perhaps just as fruitful—as my postnasal drip.

My pompous remark to my history teacher had been true: I *was* making amusing bits of order out of military chaos; and doing it was both a higher fun and a deeper satisfaction than I'd ever known. But would I be able to make a living from comic rearrangements of life? I pondered my father's annual talk to the students at Columbia's Journalism School.

"Go into advertising or public relations," he kept telling them. "You'll do better than the newspaper business, where some high school dropout like me will be sending you for coffee. And don't plan on making *The Times*: they've already got ten guys covering chess."

Anyone who could be discouraged just by his words, he told me, lacked the drive to defeat the endless discouragements of journalism itself.

"Only those kids who tell me 'Go to hell' have a chance to make it," he said.

"Well, that's the way I now feel about writing," I said, not quite able to direct him below.

"What *kind* of writing?"

"Well . . . I think I want to free-lance."   •

"Ralph, compared to free-lance writing, the newspaper business is *civil service*. Of course, if you get a *staff* job somewhere . . ."

"I don't *want* a staff job; I want to write my own stuff."

"You'll be papering your walls with rejection slips, you know."

How tired I was of hearing this trite image of a young writer's failure. How fiercely I vowed that my decor would be different. If I ever got out of the Army alive, I would sell to *The New Yorker* and paper my walls with pictures of the New York Giants.

I can do that! I kept telling myself, wondering if I could.

2

~

Did Melville Do Macy's?

Twenty-one months later, at the Headquarters of Army Forces Far East in Camp Zama, Japan, I finished writing my first book, *But I Always Called Them Sir*, a work whose most impressive literary attribute was that its pages were consecutively numbered. Less sweeping than *From Here to Eternity* or *The Cat Ate My Gymsuit*, *But I Always Called Them Sir* was a rambling though disjointed tale of a military career that fell somewhere between Benedict Arnold's and Beetle Bailey's. Its highlight, if it had one, was a recent month I had spent as an Army information man with a medical mission in East Pakistan, where I became perhaps the first soldier since Genghis Khan to simultaneously contract both dysentery and nonspecific urethritis. No hostile Chinese would have to go to the trouble of blowing off my lower half, for it was self-destructing nicely. And the irony was that this double delight came from a Chinese secretary at the U.S. Information Agency in Dacca, who often took me out to eat local ice cream and then to her home for a second dessert.

A few days after I had returned to Camp Zama and gained enough strength to walk to the post office, I mailed a carbon copy of the book to my father, who had changed his mind about my being a writer after reading the letters I had sent home, some of them with literary value because of the creative ways they asked for money. Unknown to me, my father had casually mentioned the manuscript to Louella Parsons, Hearst's Hollywood columnist, whose command of English made her the Wilma Flintstone of the American press. And then, one morning in July of 1955, just a few feet from the office of General Maxwell D. Taylor, Commander-in-Chief of Army Forces Far East, I was standing at the teletype of the International News Service and happened to read:

> Ralph Schoenstein, son of the *Journal-American's* City Editor and my friend Paul, is a Japanese corporal whose book exposing the Army, *But I Always Called Them Sarge*, will be published soon by a publisher so get to those bookstores and stay tuned!

I tried not to panic, but I failed; and less than an hour later, I was standing at fearful attention before a full colonel who also had found time to read the latest literary news from Hollywood.

"Corporal," he said with soft disgust, "I see you've written a book about the Army. That's *our* Army, I presume."

"No, sir," I said, "that column is wrong."

"You mean Louella Parsons is referring to *another* Corporal Schoenstein?"

"Colonel, the item isn't *true*. She's stupid, sir."

"You mean sorta like you? Corporal, are you aware of the regulation that men on active duty cannot write about the Army?"

"Yes, sir," I said, pleased that he had given me credit for being on active duty.

"And do you know what's happening to Colonel Voorhes for publishing that diary he kept in Korea?"

"Yes, sir, I've heard."

"Well, if we're doin' that to a bird colonel, what do you think we could do to *you*?"

"Oh, quite a bit, sir, I'm sure."

I was due to return to the States in a month for separation from service, without an intermediate five-year stop in an Army stockade; and so, I desperately repeated that Louella Parsons had a modest IQ and her transmissions were as reliable as those of Tokyo Rose.

"Look, it's right here on the INS wire," he said, "and the *Russians* didn't put it out. Schoenstein, I want to see this book."

"Sir, there *is* no book. And it hasn't been *accepted* yet."

And suddenly, I was struck by a feeling that has haunted me ever since: the dreamy absurdity of life. I was about to go to prison because of the writing of a nitwit about an imaginary event. And speaking of writing, what a splendidly absurd start for my literary career: to be jailed for publishing an unpublished book.

"Is this supposed to be a *funny* book, Corporal?" the colonel said.

"Well . . . yes and no—if it was a *book*, that is," I said, probably increasing my stockade time with my golden tongue. And now I remembered what E. B. White had said about the rewards that awaited the American humorist: *We decorate our serious writers with laurels and our wags with Brussels sprouts.* That stockade, however, wouldn't be serving me anything as tasty as Brussels sprouts.

"Corporal, by fourteen hundred today, there will be on my desk either a copy of your book or the original of your court-martial charge."

As frightened as I was, I also had a writer's detachment, which let me appreciate that this scene belonged in my book. Again I realized that what happened to me in doing my writing could be written about too, a happy truth I'd first stumbled upon three years earlier while being wheeled into surgery for a tendon repair. When the sheet covering me was removed, I had found it a challenge to keep control of both my pad and Scripto.

"You plan to do some homework in here, son?" said the surgeon, who had thought my only problem was physical.

"Then he'll want a local," the anesthetist had said.

At 0900 on the day after the colonel had read *But I Always Called Them Sir*, I returned to him, now with even more fear, for the first book review of my career.

"A piece of pure and total shit," he said. At least I had achieved an even tone. "Now Schoenstein, here's what we're gonna do. We're gonna forget a court-martial right now and just have you sign a little agreement, which says that if you publish this shit any time during your five years in the reserve, we'll call you back and find nice new quarters for you. Of course, in the meantime, if you'd like to defect to the Russians, don't let us stand in your way."

And so, bound by a deal with the Army to wait five years before I could have my first book rejected, I returned to New York and entered the world of professional writing. Using a résumé whose highlight was my editorship of the Camp Wigwam *Totem Pole*, I got a job on a Sunday supplement called *The American Weekly*, where I wrote satirical pieces that the editor kept suggesting I send to magazines that didn't care about their circulation.

"Remember what George S. Kaufman said," he told me one day. "'Satire is what closes on Saturday night.' Most Americans don't really understand it. We're a serious people who make jokes."

"But what about the sense of humor Americans are always boasting about?" I said.

"Only a people *without* a sense of humor would boast about it—a truly sophisticated one, that is. Ralph, you're doing a kind of writing that's almost as commercial as sonnets. At least *they* can be used at Hallmark. You better concentrate on the serious stuff."

"I *am* serious: this is the way I see the world."

"Well, I hope you can find an optician fast."

However, in spite of this lecture on defective American taste, the following week he sent me a manuscript about superstitions by H. Allen Smith with a note that said:

Ralph—Make this funny.

The gods of absurdity were serenading me again, for I was being asked to give humor to a celebrated humorist, to let a man with a national reputation lip-sync my latest wit. When I read H. Allen Smith's piece, it sounded as though it had been written by either Captain John Smith or Kate: although not satirical, it also managed to avoid every other known comic style. In less than a day, I wrote an entirely new one that was published under his name, a ghosting I did three more times. Therefore, the first published work of my life was under the pseudonym H. Allen Smith.

"You know this H. Allen Smith?" I said to my grandfather one day while showing him a new *American Weekly*. "Well, he's Jewish."

After making my fourth appearance as Smith, I wondered if I would soon have enough for a collection; but then the editor moved me to the sober material that he knew the American least common denominator loved: he had me ghost a story for Walter Winchell on the importance of voting, a story that, had Winchell written it, would have had a certain detachment because he never had voted. He did, however, have a pride in his work, for when I took the piece to him, he skimmed it and then smiled and said, "Kid, you tell 'em Winchell can still write."

I was now expecting Louella Parsons to tell the world:

The *Journal-American*'s City Editor Paul Schoenstein and my friend's son Ralph, currently under house arrest by the Army, has returned to the country he almost served to write under the names of Walter Winchell and H. Allen Smith. Jack London, look out!

In the fall of 1958, while I was fearing that I was destined to be just a Sunday supplement Cyrano, fortune suddenly gave me a smile bigger than Winchell's: I sold a story about my boyhood, "The Block I Lived On," to *The Saturday Evening Post*, which not only put my name on it but also paid me two thousand dollars.

Intoxicated by this stunning success, as well as by falling in love, I spent the next eight months expanding the story into a book, *The Block*, which was accepted by Random House the week that I was married. My bride was a young woman named Judy Greenspan, who had laughed out loud with questionable taste while reading *But I Always Called Them Sir*, a public school teacher who told me she wanted to be a writer.

"Keep teaching and write on the side, like Matthew Arnold and Socrates," I told her one night. "And if you do write, I hope you won't trespass on my territory the way that Zelda did to Scott."

"Well, what's your territory?" she said. "Stickball and Asian social diseases?"

Six weeks before John F. Kennedy's election, *The Block* was published as my celebration of West Side stickball, stoopball, and other bygone boyhood joys. I never dreamed, of course, that 1960-style book publishing would also become a bygone joy by 1975; for those were the days before committee-clogged conglomerates had turned publishing into a wild lust for blockbusters, the days when a lone visionary editor could play a hunch and have someone write a book that didn't have to be an instant intergalactic smash.

Because *The Block* received pleasant reviews and was actually bought by certain bookstores in carefully selected cities, I found the courage to quit *The American Weekly* and become a full-time free-lance humorist, perhaps the only mental aberration that psychiatry still does not understand. To be honest, battlefield courage wasn't needed for my leaving the magazine because Judy had a job and neither of us ate very much.

The wisdom of my flight from a tedious regular income was

clear when I sold a short satirical piece to the *Saturday Review* for twenty-five dollars. Although twenty-five dollars was one thousand, nine hundred seventy-five dollars below my customary rate, the *Saturday Review* paid in prestige; and I could feel the prestige flowing to me a few days later when Judy's college roommate called her and said, "Is Ralph working yet or is he still writing?" And I could feel it in the lobby of my apartment house the following morning when, casually attired in the nattier part of my Army uniform, I was carrying groceries to the elevator when a woman came up to me and said, "Aren't you people supposed to use the *service* entrance?"

Still more prestige flowed at a book-autographing party for me in a big New York discount store called Korvette's, where at noon one day, under a banner that said COME MEET AUTHOR RALPH SHOENSTEIN, I sat down beside fifty copies of *The Block* and waited for buyers who didn't happen to be my mother.

It was heady stuff, this first whiff of literary fame, and I planned to take the fame graciously. I had been sitting graciously beside my stack without a sale for no more than forty minutes when a woman with an apparent taste for American letters approached me and said, "Can you tell me where the scatter rugs are?"

Not everyone, of course, who stopped at my table asked about scatter rugs: one woman wanted to know if the store had a restaurant and another accidentally mentioned my book.

"*The Block?*" she said with a quizzical look. "Is it about psychiatry?"

"No," I replied, "it's about a boyhood in the city."

"Well, it looks very nice. Is it in paperback?"

"No, it's been privately printed only in this form."

"Yes, very nice. I'll have to get it at the library."

By two o'clock, I thought about autographing the scatter rugs, for they had to be moving faster than my book. By four, however, after I had gained some momentum and managed to sell an entire book every hour, two women approached me and paused nearby, beholding me as if I were something that had just come from a Chinese zoo.

"Is he the author?" one of them said.

"No, I don't think so," said the other. "If he was the author, he would have been on Jack Paar."

Although not on Jack Paar, I did play a lively little farce one morning in Macy's, where I had gone incognito to check on the book, this time with Judy's support.

"I'd like a copy of a new book called *The Block*—I hope you haven't sold out," I told a blond young man, hoping that he wouldn't recognize me as a lunatic.

"*The Block?*" he said. "Sorry, I've never heard of it. What is it, a prison story?"

"Metaphorically, yes; but on one of the other levels, it's about my boyhood. Several copies were printed in English last month. Don't you get the new books from the major publishers?"

"No, we get mostly best-sellers."

"But how do you know what's going to *be* a best-seller?" said Judy, asking a cosmic question as profound as: Where does the elephant go to die?

"Oh, the publishers tell us," he said. "Would you like the new Michener?"

At this moment, something in Judy snapped and she turned and marched all the way through the book department to the stockroom, where she tore open a dusty Random House carton and found *The Block*. Here was the essence of the romance of being married to an American writer: a woman running amok in Macy's, a woman on her knees in the stockroom, helping to take inventory.

The American system of bookselling, designed by one of the brighter members of the Jukes family, allows a store to return to the publisher all unsold books, whether or not any clerk has ever heard of them. However, philosophers often have asked: Should these books be returned in their original unopened cartons?

Pondering the internal purity of *The Block*'s distribution, Judy took some of the books, carried them to the front of the department, and put them in a prominent display of a new book on the Kennedys. *The Block* now sat beneath a sign that said:

MUST READING ABOUT AMERICA'S NEW FIRST FAMILY

It was only 1960, the start of the time of the Kennedy brothers; but I was already getting a preview of how the Ringling Brothers would be coming to book publishing.

Although *The Block* had been sold in a limited edition, and although no magazines were sending me wires requesting my work, I was able to sell myself as a satirical columnist to the Newark *Star-Ledger*, for my father, now Managing Editor of the *Journal-American*, did not want me working for him or for any competing New York paper. Having a powerful father in New York journalism had opened doors for me in New Jersey.

I was given this chance to write a humor column by Philip Hochstein, Editor-in-Chief of the Newhouse newspapers and a man of brilliance, not necessarily revealed by hiring me. On the day I walked into the *Star-Ledger* city room to talk to him about the three sample columns I had sent, he was writing an editorial on a teletype machine and he was doing only one draft, a Mozartian performance.

A few minutes later, he began our meeting with music as sweet as Mozart's: "I like the columns, Ralph. How long did it take you to write them?"

The truth was that each was a fifth or sixth or seventeenth draft; I had forgotten, but I was no Mozart. The method for writing humor almost always had to be Beethoven's: countless revisions until you felt that the lines were precisely right for producing the greatest pleasure in readers. If I had told the truth, however, about the evolution of my work to a man who put editorials on the wire first draft, he might have suggested that I do the column for a monthly.

"Not too long," I replied, for Einstein did feel that time was relative.

"Do you think you can be funny about the news five times a week?"

"Well, I'll also write about my own life. I'll mix it up."

It should have been clear that *I* was mixed up for promising an output of humor never attempted by Benchley, Thurber, Lardner, Parker, Perelman, or Buchwald. Fortunately, I had confidence to match my ignorance: I was certain that I could bring daily laughter to Newark, and parts of South Orange too.

In November of 1960, shortly after my first child, a daughter named Jill, was born, I began writing "Doubletake" for $125 a week. As a thoughtful gesture to her free-lancing father, Jill ate lightly, sometimes taking almost an hour to drink just three or four ounces of milk; and so, on my turns for feedings, I would sit beside her with a pen in my right hand and a bottle in my left, hoping that the words would flow faster than the milk. Those were among the sweetest moments I have ever known: at once filling a legal pad and a little child, dreaming that I was somehow stumbling down one or even both of the roads to immortality. No matter how absurdity might have been governing my career, those moments were not absurd, they were blessed, even when Jill and my muse simultaneously went to sleep.

By writing "Doubletake" week after week for three years, I continued to learn about the treacherous business of trying to please the American people. In one of my columns, a spoof of the stock market, I made up a few stocks that I recommended to my readers, in case I had any. About one of these tips, Feldman Oil, I said:

> The prospect for Feldman Oil seems particularly good because the company has been drilling in Texaco's fields.

Within a week after I had published this piece of insider information, the *Star-Ledger* had received more than twenty requests for the prospectus for Feldman Oil, requests that confirmed two timeless truths: the one my last colonel had taught me about people believing anything in print and the one my first editor had taught me about the sometime American sense of humor. The Feldman boom had shown that the ludicrous can be gospel for many readers, a truth whose grandest manifestation for me came twenty-five years later, when I wrote this review for *Publishers Weekly:*

In his remarkable new book, *I Never Knew Marilyn, or Joe Either, or Jim Thorpe* (Southeastern Oklahoma State University Press, 63 pages, $19.95), Newton Beatty reveals both the fullness and hollowness of America's favorite sex goddess/lost child/remedial reader better than any Marilyn Monroe biographer this entire month.

In a preface that is the highlight of this slim but not foldable work (richly adorned by photographs and box scores), Beatty is incredulous that every one of the books on Marilyn Monroe published last year missed the watershed fact that from her earliest days in Los Angeles (Was it really Los Angeles? Were they really her earliest days?), Marilyn yearned to be a metaphor. As a child, she often said to her playmates, "Now *you* be the doctor and *you* be the nurse and *I'll* be the flawed American dream."

Moreover, Beatty brilliantly notes that Marilyn married a left winger and a center fielder, but never found Mister Right.

Something deep inside her yearned to complete the trinity, but right fielders, right guards, and right tackles found her a bewildering blend of post-pubescent child and premature adult, forever pathetically seeking the Cliff's Notes for *Crime and Punishment.*

Beatty also learned that sex for Marilyn was always something else:

> Sometimes it was sex in the technical sense and some-
> times it was technique in the sexual sense, but always it
> was a poignant desire to go to sleep to continue the
> dream.

The controversial chapter, "How Old Would Marilyn
Have Been Today?" is the one in which Beatty splendidly
asserts that Marilyn was a woman when she was a little
girl, a little girl when she was a woman, and she skipped ·
her teens entirely.

> The mystery of these missing years is bound up in the
> mystery of why Marilyn's two favorite writers were Dos-
> toyevsky and Joey Adams. In every facet of her life, there
> was a similarly paradoxical duality, as if she were crying
> out, "I am antithesis! Help me!" For example, she ma-
> tured early, but was always late. She loved the Kennedys,
> but opposed the Bay of Pigs. And she hated the Yankees,
> but loved the outcome of the Civil War.

Less than twenty-four hours after this piece had appeared,
Publishers Weekly began receiving requests from bookstores and
distributors for copies of *I Never Knew Marilyn, or Joe Either, or
Jim Thorpe*. In fact, more bookstores wanted it than wanted the
books I had actually taken the trouble to put on paper. I was still
merrily working down the Rabbit Hole.

Nevertheless, by my third year of writing a column and free-
lancing to magazines, I had learned that even when my work
was being sold under the counter or was being mistaken for
Sylvia Porter, the writing was always a profound pleasure for
me, another chance to turn the dismaying jumble of life into
something perhaps entertaining and true. No matter what happens to a piece of writing, whether it is interred in Macy's or
misunderstood in Union City, you cannot take away from the
writer the pleasure of having written it; and so, I have always
pitied writers who keep saying they hate to write; for if they feel

this way, then why not do something hateful that has more security, like gun running or dermatology?

Unfortunately, lessening the pleasure of the work was the pressure of having to be funny five times a week, a pressure I handled by *not* being funny five times a week: there were columns that missed; and there also were columns that didn't miss but didn't hit like my best. I took comfort from Somerset Maugham's observation: *Only a mediocre writer is always at his best.* How skillfully I avoided mediocrity.

The mind-cracking problem of doing column after column, or figure eight after figure eight, or nose job after nose job, is that you are in constant competition with yourself and have to keep trying to top your last effort, or at least equal it.

"Today's column is okay," a friend would tell me, "but yesterday's was better. Do more like that."

Appreciating the time he had taken to make this constructive critique, I'd reply, "Who the hell asked you?"

The solution to the problem of having to keep topping yourself is to be rotten on purpose once in a while to set up a contrast that will look good.

"You have to understand the significance of the shit I wrote today," you then can say. "It's fertilizer for tomorrow."

In November of 1963, I received a call from the publisher of the *Journal-American*, J. Kingsbury Smith.

"Ralph, I'd like you to start writing 'Doubletake' for me," he said.

"Gee, I'd certainly love to," I replied, "but I'm afraid my father doesn't want me working there—the nepotism thing."

"*I'm* hiring you, not your father. I'll pay you fifty dollars for two columns a week."

Here it was at last: the chance to cut my salary by sixty percent and have my own column in the largest evening newspaper in the world. And the challenge would be unique: to keep my father from reading it.

Foolishly, Smith let him know about the new columnist and

he called me and angrily said, "You *asked Joe Smith* to come over here?"

"No, *he* called *me*—I *swear!*" I said.

"I don't know . . . I just don't know. Two Schoensteins on one paper . . ."

"You're right. You'll have to go."

Without laughing, he said, "I'll have to be very tough on you. You'll have to be twice as good as anyone else. And I *don't* want you making that column too sophisticated."

"But Pop, I'll be in *New York.*"

"Where there are just as many schmucks as anywhere else."

The following day, I told my editor at the *Star-Ledger* about my chance to move across the river.

"So your old man is giving you a column," he said with a knowing smile.

"Yes, it's the least he could do," I replied with a knowing smile at my private gods.

By late 1964, in addition to writing "Doubletake," I also had done more pieces for *The Saturday Evening Post* and the *Saturday Review,* as well as some for *Saga, Gent,* and *Dude,* three that Edmund Wilson had missed; and I had a growing pile of rejections from *The New Yorker;* elegant wallpaper was being delivered once or twice a month. I was heartened, however, to remember that *The New Yorker* had rejected the first forty or fifty submissions of the man who had kept me out of the courtroom, James Thurber.

About half of my pieces were comic looks at the life of my family, which now included a second daughter, Eve-Lynn, as lovely a miracle as Jill; and half were satirical looks at the news. Those were the days before the news was satirizing itself with such stories as Colonel Khadafy's claim that Shakespeare was an Arab, or Central State University giving a doctorate of humane letters to a half-literate heavyweight who admitted beating his wife, or Oprah Winfrey coming to grips with every family's secret fear by presenting "When Your Best Friend Marries Your

Father." In those ancient days, a satirist could still use reality as a launching pad because lunacy was not yet the American norm. No TV reporter was asking a boy who had spent his evenings attacking people in Central Park, "Tell me, what do you do for recreation?" No Vice President of the United States was telling a crowd in Bolivia, "If I'd known I was going to be spending so much time in Latin America, I would have worked harder on my Latin." And no professor of English from Northeastern University was telling a convention of the Modern Language Association, "Emily Dickinson's poems are clearly encoded images of the clitoris." When I read this professor's revelation in 1989, I regretted never having asked Mark Van Doren if Shakespeare's work was really a metaphoric cry for help from his prostate.

Putting together a variety of what seemed to be my best pieces in satire and nostalgia, I published a book called *Time Lurches On* at Doubleday, where my young editor, Tom McCormack, had perfect pitch for prose, the kind of editor who soon will be found in a case at the Smithsonian. For *Time Lurches On*, Judy decided to attack no department stores and I decided to broadcast no shopper information. Instead, while Doubleday passed up all advertising to invest heavily in word-of-mouth, Judy and I enjoyed the reviews, and also deeply gratifying letters from Mark Van Doren, Jerome Weidman, and P. G. Wodehouse, who recommended me to *Punch* with a kindness that matched his comic gift.

And then came what every writer dreams of: recognition by *The New York Times Book Review*; and mine was a dream by Dali, for it transcended mere disapproval. In a remarkable display of concise writing, a man named Herbert Mitgang managed to squeeze five errors of fact into a four-hundred-word review of *Time Lurches On*. As a critic, he had the right, of course, to call my book something that should be recycled. He had *no* right, however, to review what I had not written: to say, for example, that he disliked my quoting David Susskind or my passage on Hearst cartoons. The book contained not one line about Susskind or Hearst or any cartoon. The cartoon was *The Times* reviewer, who either hadn't read the whole book or else had read the whole book with a wee intellect.

The Block had been overlooked by *The New York Times*, so this was my first literary appearance in America's newspaper of record; and the review enriched what was already my distinctive literary tradition: it was absurd, a theme that was as much in my working life as in my material.

Thus had I learned early in my career what writers through the ages have had to learn: how it felt to be attacked by someone who based his views more on his own bitterness than on your book. The review, in fact, was such inept reporting that it had its own comic peaks, one of which was Mitgang saying:

> Echoes abound of Uncle Miltie, Fibber McGee, Leonard Lyons, Jimmy Cannon, Arthur Murray, and the humor columnists on the *Journal-American*.

How *did* Arthur Murray sound? Like a pair of pumps on a ballroom floor? And what was the collective sound of the humor columnists on the *Journal-American*, where I was the only one? Mitgang had accused me of sounding like myself.

On a deeper level, or perhaps a shallower one, he had made the great mistake that E. B. White had warned about: judging humor by its so-called importance, for he felt that my subject matter was "sadly limited." In a way, of course, he was right: my subject matter *was* limited: to only childhood, psychoanalysis, tipping, a Jewish boy's Christmas, the poignance of the New York Giants, explosions of jargon, expurgated fairy tales, condensations of symphonies, my life as a wounded bull on Wall Street, sweet memories of oldtime radio, God's uncertain place in America, the fight for the air rights over Grant's Tomb, an adventure in unemployment insurance, the birth of a book, the day the sun didn't rise, the terror of New Year's Eve, the terrors of summer camps, and a merry tour of the three different tombs of Christopher Columbus.

"I'm going to kill him," I told Judy. "It's the only intelligent response."

"It would probably be better not to," she said. "I'm sure he's just a little man who would rather be writing books than reviewing them."

"The one thing I don't need now is perspective."

"On top of which, he's a knee-jerk liberal who's still fighting Hearst and that's kind of quaint: he's twenty years out of date."

"All that may be true. But just for fun, I'm going to kill him."

"Well, all right, if you really *want* to. You're a free-lance humorist, so the judge will have to accept an insanity plea."

I settled, however, for writing a long angry letter to *The Times* that discussed the rotten reporting on its way to microfilm; and a few weeks later, the letter was published, followed by Mitgang's brief explanation of what he had meant by one of his mistakes. His tacit confession was satisfying, but it didn't repair the damage, for American bookstores and libraries based their orders on *The New York Times Book Review*, not on *Seventeen*.

Mitgang's review left me shaken because it was a literary hat trick: dishonest, mean-spirited, and unfair. Of course, John F. Kennedy had reminded me that life itself was unfair, and then had become a definitive example of the point. Moreover, *Time Lurches On* did receive many good reviews; a British critic called it "impeccable prose," but I couldn't stop seething about the one that was not fit to print. And suddenly, I decided that I would never read another review of my work, for the good ones didn't praise me enough and the bad ones hurt too much. For the pain of this one, I found balm by remembering what Haydn had said to a young composer: "They never built a statue to a critic."

And if they *did*, Haydn probably thought, we would have to start raising pigeons.

In the following days, while I tried to lose myself in my column and also a piece about outdoor concerts for the *Saturday Review*, I could not help but ponder the script of my life, which seemed to have been written either by Beckett or Mr. Magoo, and was in such ironic contrast to my intention to give life order, sense, and sparkle in my work. I had no inkling, of course, that just ahead for me were two literary adventures— one that would lead to a President's doghouse, the other to a Chicago jail—so surrealistic as to make my entire past in publishing seem like A *Child's Garden of Verses*.

ENTR'ACTE

Humor can be dissected, as a frog can, but the thing dies in the process. Humor has a certain fragility, an evasiveness, which one had better respect.

With these words of E. B. White haunting me, I now will nervously raise my scalpel and do some dissecting that White might have called malpractice, for I cannot resist saying some things between the tales of my misadventures that I have learned about this fragile and evasive view of life.

Here comes the first dying frog.

In the summer of 1970, to prove I was au courant about more than just the Munich agreement, I began writing for *National Lampoon*, a new humor magazine that was a version of the *Harvard Lampoon*. Although *National Lampoon* did break new ground, it eventually moved to no ground at all, to a swamp of material that ranged from the merely offensive to the godawful. A revolution in humor instead had turned revolting, for the *Lampoon's* young editors felt that the soul of wit was shock and they were moved to capture all the merriness of Dachau, cancer, and the Mai Lai massacre. After having written three pieces for the magazine—a spoof of the sexual revolution, a salute to old money, and a parody of *The Gift of the*

Magi—I was suddenly embarrassed to appear in it, and I was a man who had been appearing in the bosom of *Playboy*. But enormous bare breasts were the heart of good taste, so to speak, when weighed against what the *Lampoon* now was printing. Feeling a bit biblical, in May of 1971 I went to the publisher, Matty Simmons, planning to give him a lesson in aesthetics, for I was certain I knew what humor was. My work was already in five anthologies, and two of them were being used in college English classes. The lesson, however, turned out to be one given to me.

"Matty," I said, "you're running stories that make me cringe. I've just never been able to find much humor in cancer and murdered kids. I can't imagine who does."

"All the people who pay your fees," he replied. "Take a look at our sales in the colleges. The kids *love* this stuff; it's the new humor."

"It's *no* humor and what the kids love is no standard. The kids also love wet dreams, which is next month's cover story, I guess."

"I didn't know we had a house rabbi. You can start blessing the Danish."

"Matty, it's not just the subjects, it's the *execution*. Maybe I'm wrong; maybe *any* subject can be done; but it's got to be heightened by *wit*, by some kind of *style*. Your Harvard boys think it's funny just to say 'Fuck Mother Teresa.' Well, I'm afraid 'Fuck Mother Teresa'—if that's your latest burst of the new humor—needs something else; and don't ask me what."

"Let me get this straight. *You're* the authority on what's funny?"

"Of *course* not: humor is a matter of taste; but your boys don't happen to have any. I mean, it's all subjective, but there are still absolutes, if you'll pardon my Zen."

"No question about it, Ralph," he said with a maddening smirk. "And Disraeli felt the same way: no jokes about Queen Victoria, religion, or sex. Okay, you can be our house Victorian too and make sure we don't offend anyone at Ascot."

"Matty, *I'm* no prude: hell, *I* did our sex spoof; but what exactly is the satirical point in spoofing the Holocaust? Look, no matter how original art is—and it *has* to be original, of course—it still needs *intelligence* behind it. Even being entertainingly *tasteless* requires taste."

"Nonsense; the stuff is just off-the-wall."

"If stuff comes off the wall, it still has to touch the ground. To move from handball to tennis, your boys are playing without a net."

"They should throw a net over *you*. Do you know how much *money* this magazine makes?"

It had seemed to me at the time that I could have been having an equally rewarding discussion by exploring aesthetics with Porky Pig; but years later I realized that I had been even thicker than Matty; for instead of trying to shape the *Lampoon* to my taste, I simply should have folded my sermon and slipped away, muttering "*De gustibus non est disputandum.*"

What a jerk, that Disraeli. Couldn't he have seen what a splendid subject for satire Queen Victoria was? I was glad that my grandfather hadn't collected *him*.

3

~

He's with the Dogs

On All Fools Day, 1965, a man named G. Daniel Kramer called me and asked if I wanted to write a book about Lyndon Johnson's dogs.

"I package books," he said, sounding like a wrapper in Womrath's, "and this one has me in heat because it's absolutely got it *all*. People love dogs and they love Johnson; just look at the polls. You know, he even takes them to *church*—the dogs, not the polls."

I laughed while trying to think quickly. The ideas for the two books I'd already written had come from me, the ideal source; but here was a chance to play off the Presidency. I didn't know what the latest polls were saying about love for dogs, but I knew that Lyndon Johnson had more than sixty percent of the nation's affection. He demanded it.

"Gee," I said, not yet in heat but warming to the idea, "a book like that *could* be something . . . sort of a heartwarming two-cushion shot. It could even start *off* in church: a kind of canine cantata."

I silently apologized to Mark Van Doren.

"That's good language, Ralph," said Dan Kramer, responding to my mangy metaphor. "Johnson takes those dogs to church, to the office—*everywhere*. A guy at the White House told me he practically *lives* with them and nobody knows about it. Hell, Blanco's had almost *no* publicity. Most people think the other beagle's still alive: they don't know that he died and was replaced by Blanco."

"Who's Blanco?"

"A white collie. See? He's getting no press. I tell you, these dogs can be *had*."

"Wow," I said as my mind shifted into low and I saw the fortune to be made by *The Baptism of LBJ's Beagle*.

"I've already talked to Lady Bird's press secretary, Liz Carpenter, and the White House'll cooperate. We'd have the exclusive story of the dogs *with* pictures. What say, Ralphie?"

"The only thing is . . . Well, I may not be the right man for dogs. I own a cat and five dead caterpillars."

Jill had recently brought six caterpillars home from the park. Five were now in butterfly heaven and one was somewhere in my bed.

"Look, at least let's go down there and touch bases. Then just knock out an outline and I *know* a publisher'll grab it for plenty. You don't have to go the pure Lassie route: you could do a dog's-eye view of the news. *You* know: what the dogs think about Israel, Vietnam, and stuff like that."

"I'm afraid that's kind of corny, Dan. And how would *I* know what the dogs think of the news? I mean, I'd have to fake it. In a book like that, you'd get more of *my* opinions than the dogs'."

"Steady, boy. I just mean their reactions to famous people and events—*dog* reactions—might be one cute way to do it; but you'd be free to go any route you want. And you'd have fifty percent of the whole package."

Here indeed was the knock of opportunity: Kramer was offering me a half interest in my own book. It wasn't *every* writer who received an offer like that.

"I could've hired a writer for a flat fee," he said, "but you're a beautiful language man and the dogs'll really need styling. So at least think about it, okay?"

Only moments after agreeing to do so and then hanging up, I had thought enough to be struck by the grandeur of the idea: a writer just *couldn't miss* with a book about a President and his dogs! Even if you were a *homely* language man, such a book would still be as popular as tax evasion. Dizzy with the thought of an orbital flight from the lower middle class, I roughly added the number of Johnson votes in the '64 landslide to the audience of *Lassie*; and then, after talking to Judy, I called Dan back and accepted the deal. He happily said he would write a partnership contract saying that he had the final word in all business affairs and I was in charge of everything shaggy.

Four days later, the former Mr. H. Allen Smith went to Washington.

At the outside sentry booth of the White House, Dan announced us, showed the guard a credit card for identification, and I flashed a membership in the YMHA. After clearing us, the guard told someone in the East Wing that we were coming to see Mrs. Carpenter. And he also might have added to watch me closely, for Dan had a hat, vest, and attaché case, but I had only a wash-and-wear suit with a neat little stain of Baby Magic on one of the sleeves.

About five minutes later, a smiling young woman came down a staircase to us and said, "Hi! You must be Mr. Kramer and Mr. Schoenfeld. I'm Marcia Maddox. We're all terribly excited about your book."

With the elegantly bubbly air of a Bryn Mawr pledge in the Peace Corps, she led us to the second-floor office of the Press Secretary to Mrs. Lyndon B. Johnson; and there we met Elizabeth Carpenter, a chubby woman who told us in the tones of Texas, "The dogs belong to Luci; I don't really know much about 'em." And she was telling no lie: in a recent interview, she had called the beagle Him "that bitch."

"May I talk to Luci?" I said, planning to start small and work my way up to Dad.

"Oh, no," she said quickly, "Luci can't be interviewed. You can get all you need from Mr. Bryant; he takes care of the dogs. Marcia, have Mr. Bryant come up."

While the keeper of the hounds was on his way, Liz told us how "charmin'" she felt this book could be.

"Yes, it'll make the President look good," I said. "Create a lot of warm feeling towards him."

"And we'll work right along with you. We'll check the whole manuscript before it comes out."

A few minutes later, Dan and I were standing in the Rose Garden with Traphes Bryant, who'd been telling us how much time LBJ spent with Him and Blanco. Pointing to the French door of Johnson's office, he said, "Why, they've already been in there with him for three hours today."

Across twenty yards of lawn, I strained to see through the door; and suddenly, I *saw* it: the back of the President of the United States. I had once met Phil Rizzuto, but this was clearly a new high.

"The President really loves those animals," said Bryant. "He just about lives with 'em."

And then he spun some tender tales about America's First Dogs: for example, that Blanco was a junkie.

"We got 'im on tranquilizers. He's kind of a nervous wreck."

"Well, the buck stops here," I said, "and I guess it's just too much pressure for him. What kind of tranquilizers does he take?"

"Look, you can't go printin' any *brand* names. We can't have the White House endorsin' *dope*."

"Oh, of *course* not. I mean, this book won't be called *All Creatures Great and Stoned*."

Already, with mounting delight, I could see the book it *was* going to be: a sympathetic new view of the President's personal life. In too many recent stories, LBJ had been painted as a vain and ruthless man; but *this* story would be a touching revelation of his hidden humanity, even though that humanity was clearer to another species.

"Mr. Bryant, I'll be wanting a three-dimensional picture of man *and* beast, so can you really give me all the dirt on these dogs? I don't want to get you in trouble with . . ." I looked towards the Big Back.

"Oh, don't worry," he said. "I'm Civil Service."

"Could Mr. Kramer and I see the dogs before we leave?"

"Yes, I'll be takin' 'em for a walk in about ten minutes."

When he finally went in and brought out the dogs, I tried to see signs of their having just spent three hours at the feet of the most important man in the world; but I could see only a high-strung collie and a playful beagle who licked my hand. Standing there, I tried hard to feel the awesome stickiness of it all.

On the plane returning to New York, I suddenly turned to Dan as if I had just seen the wing on fire.

"Dan, we're *not* going to clear this book with *Liz Carpenter*, are we?"

"Of course not," he said. "If we do show it to her, it'll be just as a courtesy. She won't have the right to make any changes."

"Well, I think she *does* expect to approve the book before it's printed and we don't want this to be a PR handout for Johnson."

"Relax; she'll love it."

"Dan, it's a bad idea to give press agents a chance to approve copy—even presidential ones. And that dame seems a little dizzy to me anyway. In fact, the whole office is like a sorority at SMU."

"For Crissake, will you *relax*! No one down there is gonna fool around with your integrity. *You* know I won't let anyone rape you; I have too much respect for your work. So just relax; we're gonna swing with this whole package. Do you realize the *fallout* that this thing could have? Him and Blanco T-shirts, board games, comic books—the whole route." He laughed financially. "Dad, it could be bigger than James Bond: we could make the whole *country* go doggie! And that could mean forty or fifty grand apiece for us—even *more* if we get a movie."

"Just imagine," I said as if in prayer. "The whole country gone doggie."

"Of course, for the movie, we'll have to stick some kinda story into the book, maybe something about a little boy who comes to the White House fence to see the dogs."

"We could call it *Boy at the Fence.*"

"Hey, that's *language.* You just keep writing like that and I'll keep the White House happy."

The following morning, I wrote a short outline:

HIM AND BLANCO—A STORY OF THE PRESIDENT'S DOGS

(Boy at the Fence)

Day and night, the President of the United States conducts an enchanting love affair with two dogs: a beagle named Him and a rare white collie named Blanco.

These two dogs are Lyndon Johnson's joy and even therapy. When he is at his desk, they are often with him, either curled at his feet or on his couch—and sometimes chewing his rug. They go with him on walking press conferences around the White House lawn, leaving him only to chase an occasional squirrel up a tree. They fly with him in jets to Austin and in helicopters to Camp David; they swim in the White House fountains; they romp with the world's VIPs; and at night, they sometimes flop on the bed of America's First Lady.

Not only does LBJ love these dogs, but he shares them with thousands of visitors who come to the White House fence to admire and even pet them. This book will tell the story of one small boy who comes often to the fence and develops a touching relationship with the dogs. Eventually, his two friends lure him inside and all three share a great adventure in the White House, an adventure that will combine timeless charm with timely news in a rare appeal for young and old.

Just one or two small details in the narrative still had to be worked out: for example, how the boy could get through the fence without being arrested, electrocuted, or shot. A shooting, however—just a wounding, of course—might have led to a lovely scene in which the President went to the boy's bedside and said, both dramatically and grammatically, "Get well quickly, son, for me and Him."

While I pondered such artistic challenges, Dan sent the outline to Ken McCormick, Editor-in-Chief of Doubleday, my publisher, who accepted it at once for a ten-thousand-dollar advance. During the publication of *Time Lurches On*, Ken had been high on my work, even though he had felt that the time had not yet come to share it with the public.

When the first half of the advance reached Dan, I drew only fifteen hundred dollars from my share, for Judy was still bringing home a teacher's salary, and Dan and I wanted to save all we could for big expenses: trips to Washington, a photographer's fee, and assorted bribes.

We made our second trip to the White House on a splendid April day: the south lawn tulips were aflame and so was my curiosity about the dogs. I kept pumping Bryant for details of their life with LBJ and he gave me one delightful story after another, stories never before told, such as the one about Him curled up in a blanket of military secrets on the bed of the Commander-in-Chief.

I'd been making notes for about twenty minutes when Marcia Maddox came out and said, "*Hi*, Mr. Schoenbrun! Listen, I have a *swell* source of material for your book on the White House ceremonies."

After gently correcting her and then introducing myself, I mentioned the interview I had requested with the President.

"Oh, that's out of the question!" she said. "You can't interview the President about *dogs*! And listen, I just saw one of your books—that *Time Latches On*—and I certainly hope that *this* one isn't supposed to be funny too. The Presidency is just too . . . *significant* to be humorous."

"Well . . . merry significance, I hope," I said as I remembered the words of Louis Kronenberger that sat on my desk:

> . . . the truly insane theory that what is amusing must be less significant than what is ponderous or grim, that what is witty must be more superficial than what is sober, that what is fanciful contains less truth than what is factual.

While I was reluctantly returning from Kronenberger's depths to Marcia's light-headedness, LBJ and the press corps suddenly came marching across the lawn, a parade encircled by Secret Service men.

"Let's go over to the President," said Bryant to my delight. "He always wants the dogs with him out here."

And so, the White House canine correspondent trotted towards the President. I was less than twenty yards away when a Secret Service agent slammed a hand on my shoulder and said, "Mister, who are *you?*"

"Oh, *he's* okay," said Bryant. "He's with the dogs."

Perhaps only one other American writer, perhaps only Henry David Thoreau, would have been pleased to have as his references a couple of animals.

For the next ten minutes, I marched around just a few feet from the President; and I knew how suspicious I must have looked, for all the other writers had their eyes on LBJ, but *I* was watchiing the dogs. It was like going into the Sistine Chapel to gaze at the floor.

All through the spring, I worked on the book, drawing a minimum from the kitty. Our photographer was shooting at the White House for two hundred dollars a day, Dan had lubricated

Bryant with a case of bourbon, and I had made three more trips to the dogs. By June, I had finished a second draft of *Boy at the Fence*, a book with a quality unique in American letters; it was a satirical, fantastical, fictional documentary too political for children and too preposterous for adults.

"It touches all bases," said Dan.

"Yes, a triple play," I said. "The only thing missing is recipes."

Dan was eager to sell the book to Hollywood, but I feared it could never become a movie because it had all the narrative power of *The World Almanac*. It was fragile fact-fiction that may not have worked even in print.

"This isn't exactly *Ben Hur*," I told him. "Most of the action is mental, so they'd have to film my mind."

"Don't worry," he replied, "I know I can swing with it out there."

On Friday the thirteenth of August, I sent a third draft of the book to Ken McCormick; and ten days later, he wrote:

Dear Ralph:

I read *Boy at the Fence* with great admiration. You've taken a subject which could have been thoroughly bitched up and made that rarest of literary commodities: a unique book. This look at a lonely man at the top, with two of man's best friends, is endearing, amusing, and moving.

We're going into Sales Conference in early September and it's going to be a pleasure to tell the men about this enchanting book. I'm going to tell them that Ralph Schoenstein as a property has grown by leaps and bounds, and that you're the H. Allen Smith of Doubleday's next decade. Congratulations!

Yours,
Ken

P.S. I do feel a few small cuts will broaden the reading audiences.

When I went to Ken's office the following day, I was so giddy from his response that I couldn't bring myself to tell him that I already had *been* H. Allen Smith, though I still hadn't been Robert Frost or Pearl Buck. After praising me again, he said that he wanted just four lines cut from the sixty-six-page manuscript. I cut all four right there at his desk and the book then went to a copy editor.

As I was leaving Ken's office, his assistant, Stan Marks, said, "Ralph, I just can't *tell* you how much we like your book. You know, I've always hated Johnson, but for the first time I feel some sympathy for him."

"Gee . . . thanks," I replied.

"The book has so many *levels;* we don't even know how to describe it to the salesmen. It's even got an undercurrent of *Mondo Cane.*"

I didn't know what the hell he was talking about, so I gave him an inscrutable smile and said, "I'm glad you caught that. There may also be a bit of *Bob, Son of Battle* too."

"I shouldn't tell you this," he said softly, "but do you know the sales projection on your book?"

"Four ninety-five?"

"No, I mean the *number* we plan to sell."

"Well, one to every American would be nice."

"Ralph, the projection is a hundred thousand copies."

I wasn't surprised: I *always* had aimed for a hundred thousand sales. *Time Lurches On* had fallen just ninety-seven thousand short.

When Dan heard about this sales projection, he felt confirmed in his feeling that we would be offering Hollywood a flea-bitten *Gone With the Wind;* but I hadn't lost *my* feeling that it would have been easier to film *The Yellow Pages.*

"*Please* don't go to Hollywood," I told him. "Let's just concentrate on the literary stuff: the magazine pickups, book clubs, and Johnson dolls. Besides, they've already *made Mondo Cane.*"

"Down boy," he replied. "Look, I've got Disney and a dozen others panting for this thing." He was lost in a linguistic kennel. "By the way, bring a copy to my office so I can send it to Liz."

"*No!* Dan, you *promised* that—"

"Relax, it's just a courtesy to set up the movie."

Three days later, Doubleday's copy editor finished the book and asked me to change just two words in the twenty thousand. I did so, the book went off to be designed, and Dan received the second half of our advance. *Boy at the Fence* had officially been accepted by Doubleday and scheduled for high-speed publication under a new name: *Him, Blanco, and LBJ*, a title that moved the book back towards nonfiction. Him's bed may have been classified, but his story was unclassifiable.

As Dan flew to Disneyland, I smiled at the thought of how *this* one would be coming into Macy's: in cartons opened at once, perhaps by the National Guard, and then in great stacks under the banner:

MUST READING ABOUT AMERICA'S
FOUR-FOOTED FIRST FAMILY

4

~

Down, Ralphie!

One afternoon the following week, while Hanoi was being bombed and Watts was being torn apart and my couch was being destroyed by my cat, the telephone rang and I suddenly heard, "Mr. Schoenstein, this is Liz Carpenter."

"Yes, how are you?" I said, prepared for Potomac praise of my work.

"Well, I can't say I'm *happy*. I've read this so-called book of yours and it's just *impossible*. There's somethin' on every *page* that makes the President look foolish."

As an example, she quoted a line on page 2 that spoofed Richard Nixon. When I asked her for other examples of anti-LBJ prose, she said, "Well, I haven't read the *whole* book, but it's *full* of 'em."

"How much *have* you read?"

"The first six pages; but I know the rest is just as bad. The girls are in a state of collapse."

That didn't seem to be the best position for them to work in;

but it wasn't my place to tell this woman how to run her office when she was still trying to achieve a third grade concentration span, and when she was having such heartbreaking difficulty telling the difference between Nixon and Johnson.

"Look," she said, "you'd better come right on down here and we'll rewrite the book from scratch because *this* way it can't be printed. I absolutely won't approve it."

"Well, I'm sorry to disagree," I said, once again incredulously feeling myself being sucked into a dopey dream, "but *I* think it's a very favorable portrait of the President. I'll bet he would *love* it."

"Mr. Schoenstein, if the President ever knew that I'd been part of something like this, he'd tell me to go straight to hell." It was a message she richly deserved. "Look, this is supposed to be a picture book, isn't it?"

"No, the pictures are sec—"

"So you just come on down here right away and I'll help you re-do the words—if you want the book to come out, that is."

For at least a minute after putting down the phone, I sat in silent nausea and saw whole warehouses of T-shirts and dolls go up in smoke. I saw the whole country going gerbil. And then I asked myself: Did a White House press agent have any *right* to make changes in the book, even *sensible* ones? The question, of course, was rhetorical.

By the time that I was able to talk to Dan in Beverly Hills, I had decided that we would just have to ignore Carpenter and all her collapsible ladies, for we didn't *need* her approval. Disney could build his *own* White House.

When I told Dan about the way she had panicked, he said we would simply go to Washington and calm her down.

"She doesn't sound calmable," I told him. "Dan, the woman sees English as a foreign language."

"Dad, she has absolutely no say in this thing."

"Of *course*, but you'd still better come right back. She's made herself my collaborator and I think we're doing a pop-up book."

*   *   *

At five o'clock on the afternoon of September 24, the telephone brought me a message of biblical simplicity:

"Ralph, this is Ken. We're in trouble: Liz hates the book."

"I know," I said; "she called me. So she won't buy a copy. I
mean, we don't have to please Lady Bird's press agent. Ken, she
has no *right* to make any changes: we don't *need* her approval."

"That's true; and ordinarily, I'd tell her to go to hell. But you
see, Ralph, we have . . . we have some pretty big things going
for us down there. I don't have to spell it out for you."

Spelled out, it would have read O-T-H-E-R B-O-O-K-S.

"But we can't turn the book into a press release for *Johnson.*
Ken, *she's* not my editor, *you* are!"

"Yes, of course; but I'm afraid you'll still have to go down
there and see what changes she wants."

"But the woman's *crazy!* She read only *six pages* and she
didn't understand *those!*"

"Yes, I know. Johnson has them a bit overtrained down
there. But unless you can make the changes she wants, or at
least find a way to make her happy, I'm afraid we can't do the
book."

It was a simple enough request: do Ken a favor or let Doubleday cancel my contract, a contract that had no clause about
approval by any of Lyndon's little women.

Three days later, I received a letter from Ken reminding me
of my agreement to clear the book with Liz, an agreement I had
trouble remembering because it didn't exist. Ken said that Liz
had written to Dan in August about expecting to see the book;
and thus Doubleday was basing its case on an *ex post facto*
agreement between Liz and herself, *ex post facto* because the
book contract had been signed in April.

A few minutes after getting this letter, I was on the phone
with Ken, who said, "At least see what changes she wants. At
least *try* to compromise with her. Keep an open mind."

"Damn *right* I will!" I said.

I was fired up, for Dan had told me, "You're being raped, Dad, and that doesn't happen to writers I work with."

I *hoped* not: the last two writers he had worked with were Ruth Montgomery and Bette Davis.

Dan and I decided to see Liz on October 4, the day of the Pope's visit to New York, for the Johnsons would be in New York until evening and she would have time to discuss all the corrections with us. On October 3, however, Ken called me with news that he felt might affect our meeting:

"Ralph, Liz just told me that she's not interested in making *any* revisions."

"Neither am I," I said. "We finally agree."

"*You* know what I mean: I'm afraid she doesn't want it published at all."

"No, I think we disagree on that."

"I'm so glad you're taking all this in good spirit; I know what an inconvenience it must be. But please don't break your date with her just because she doesn't want to see you. She's just a bit overtrained."

"You mean like the dogs."

He laughed again. "In fact, you want to hear something silly? She's got the Secret Service checking on you and Dan."

While I prepared for a creative conference with a woman who wanted my book buried at sea, a woman whose extra training had taught her that a jab at Nixon wounded Johnson, I pondered my curiouser and curiouser state. I had written a happy, affectionate book about the loving heart of the President of the United States and Doubleday had liked it enough to plan on a hundred thousand sales. I was on my way to a resurgence as H. Allen Smith; but suddenly, women were collapsing, the Secret Service was digging, and Nelson Doubleday was singing "Let that dog book go." Was all this really happening in America, where Lyndon Johnson had just signed a bill to aid the arts? I had heard of White House news management, but never *veterinary* news. Did my book give military secrets or tell of lust in the Lincoln bedroom? No, it contained only such momentous revelations as:

On Him's collar was a tag saying LBJ FOR THE USA.

When Dan and I walked into Liz's office for our surrealistic summit, she wasted no time with pre-censorship small talk.

"This would be *awful* to print," she said, giving me the marked-up manuscript. "It's just *full* of things that're undignified and untrue—things that would make the President look *terrible* all over the world. I mean, the Voice of America would end up *apologizin'* for this book!"

I could hear the faint strains of "Columbia, the Gem of the Ocean" and I suddenly knew how Benedict Arnold must have felt at the end.

"For instance," she said, "you got Him chewin' up the rug in the Oval Office. Well, that just never happened."

"I'm sorry," I replied, "but Mr. Bryant said it did."

"Well, you've got Blanco on tranquilizers and you just can't *write* things like that about a President's dog."

"Why not? Are you afraid of mail from the Lassie lobby?"

"Believe me, we'd get mail about this book. Why, you even got one line in there about the dogs runnin' the *country.*"

"I suspect that most readers will know that they're not," I said, thinking of Feldman Oil. "That line won't be taken seriously by anyone with a measurable IQ."

"Well, just look at all those *other* things I caught." And turning to Dan, she said, "I don't know *who* ever told this man he was qualified to write about dogs. He's with the Hearst papers, isn't he?"

Taking a few minutes now to quickly look through the sixty-six pages, I saw that only twelve had been untouched by her patriotic pencil. She did, however, give consideration to the book's continuity by never killing more than one paragraph on any single page.

The opening lines of the book were:

At his desk in the White House sat the 36th President of the United States. On a couch nearby lay one of his most treasured friends. The friend was Him, not a god but a beagle who'd been Lyndon Johnson's constant companion for the past two years . . .

Liz cut the word "god" and wrote in "reporter," thus drawing her first mustache on my work.

On page 2, she cut an entire subversive paragraph that began:

The bond between the dog on the couch and the man at the desk was like the one between FDR and Fala . . .

On page 3, in a passage on the death of the beagle Her, there were seven cuts and a mind-numbing revision of this line:

Him got sacks of condolence cards and the White House was bombarded by offers of pets.

Liz had cut "bombarded" and put in "beseized," which, if intended to be English, probably meant "to be seized by a bee" and should have been used only for pollen.

On page 6, she cut a quote by Johnson that had come from the Associated Press; and on page 7, she cut this whole passage:

This masseur was the man who'd been damned for hoisting Him by the ears, the greatest howling about a pet since the charge that FDR had sent a destroyer to bring Fala from the South Pacific. To many Americans, an ear lift was worse than a sea lift. However, there had *been* no ear lift: LBJ had simply put his hands under the back of Him's front legs to raise him for pictures and the hands had slipped to his ears. But the hind legs had never left the ground.

Here Liz at last had caught me in a mistake. As a courtesy to the President, I had told the White House version of this story and it was a charming little fiction. Incredibly, Liz had cut a lie that I'd used to make her boss look good. My cherry tree had been chopped down by a Carpenter's axe.

By page 21, I had found six cuts of facts about Johnson that I had taken from *The New York Times,* as well as a cut of this last line of chapter one:

Then Him and Blanco followed their best friend into his office and lay down near his desk while he brooded about atoms being split by Mao Tse-tung.

Of all the changes in the book, fifty-four pages of shimmering stupidity, this one bewildered me most. To what was Liz objecting? That the dogs lay near the President's desk? That the President brooded? Or that Mao Tse-tung had the bomb? She had entered an area of Zen editing.

When I finally looked up from the manuscript, I said, "Mrs. Carpenter, all these corrections . . . well, I'm afraid they're just *silly:* they just don't make any *sense.*"

"If the boys in the West Wing ever saw this," she said, "they'd drop dead. You gotta present the President with *dignity.*"

"But it's a warm, happy picture of him—*three-dimensional*— and the President really *needs* this kind of human picture right now; the papers are printing Messiah jokes about him. Here, read this from my editor."

As if playing a trump, I dropped Ken's letter on her desk, the letter that said, ". . . that rarest of literary commodities: a unique book."

She read it and then said, "Well, this must be a very young and irresponsible man."

I smiled like a benign executioner. "He's the Editor-in-Chief of the biggest publishing house in America."

"Then he's a *nut.* Look, this just isn't the book you were *supposed* to write. Why don't you take out all the political stuff and just use the story about the little boy?"

"I'm afraid you've forgotten our original outline," said Dan, putting it before her.

She glanced at it as if it were something she wanted to swat. "Mr. Kramer, I want you both to know something. My loyalty isn't to Doubleday or dog lovers: it's to the President of the United States!"

I felt an urge to salute something; but instead I said, "Listen, we all have plenty of time today and I'm really not inflexible. Why don't we go over your changes page by page and see if we can work these things out?"

"Oh, I couldn't do that," she said. "Gwen Cafritz is expecting me for cocktails."

All during the flight back to New York, I kept studying an incredible thing: a censored book about dogs. I now had the option of considering all of Liz's changes and then making them.

"I won't let you be raped," said Dan. "We've got to hang tough; we still can swing."

"That's just what they said to John Brown," I replied.

In the days that followed, while Dan reviewed our case with a lawyer, I wondered if there was any chance for the book to be published at more than fifteen pages. I grew to hate the sight of beagles; and when Him became a father, I didn't even send a card.

Late one afternoon near the end of October, despair drove me to make a phone call to Ken's assistant, Stan Marks, and I asked him to meet me right away outside the office because I was considering going mad. He agreed; and a few minutes later, we met at a coffee shop on East 68th Street, just around the corner from a synagogue and the New York headquarters of the FBI, both of which I was planning to use.

After hearing my outrage, Stan said, "Ralph, they're giving you the business, but you should still try your damndest to compromise. For your own sake, *don't* get into a fight with Nelson Doubleday."

"Why?" I said. "What does he weigh?"

"Well, he swings enough weight so he just killed the first biography of Malcolm X, the Black Muslims' top guy. It's a terrific book and it's already in *galleys.*"

"Then he must want something bigger, like the memoirs of Haile Selassie or Sammy Davis, Jr. Stan, you seem to be forgetting that I happen to be legally and morally *right.*"

"Of *course* you are; and if you threatened to sue, we'd have to print the book, but we'd just print a few hundred copies and hide them in a warehouse. That's what Nelson's father did when he killed one of Theodore Dreiser's books because his wife didn't like it."

"Gee, it's nice to be part of a fine old tradition."

"And I'll tell you something else, but if you quote me, I'll deny it."

I laughed. "I never thought I'd hear a line like that outside the movies. But this one feels more like Looney Tunes than Hitchcock."

He laughed too. "Yes, I know it sounds ridiculous, but right now we're also giving the business to Clark Mollenhoff."

"For attacking baseball, right? Nelson's great-grandfather, Abner?"

"He's doing a book that criticizes McNamara."

"The White House says you can't criticize McNamara?"

"Only favorably."

"Look, Stan, it's comforting to know that Doubleday always publishes like *Pravda,* but that still doesn't *help* me. So I want you to take a message to Ken and Nelson and the boys in the mailroom too: tell 'em this book is gonna come out the way I *wrote* it, and if I have to sell it from a warehouse or a *whorehouse,* then that's what I'll do! Goddammit, this isn't the fucking *Third Reich!*"

In my rage, I had mixed my fascisms, for the Third Reich didn't publish *Pravda,* but otherwise my head was clear and so was my goal: I would *not* be the Dreyfus of dog literature.

*   *   *

The ultimatum I sent through Stan had an instant effect on Doubleday: the following morning, it postponed indefinitely the publication of *Him, Blanco, and LBJ*. Doubleday would not be telling America about either a Black Muslim or a white collie.

At once, Dan began showing the book to other houses; and within a week, it was accepted by Lippincott, a house with no yen for the memoirs of Johnson's gardener, plumber, or proctologist. My despair had suddenly turned to hope, for the book would be printed the way I had written it—*if* Doubleday would release it to me. I decided, therefore, to make a personal appeal to Ken: on the Saturday before Thanksgiving, he took me to lunch at the Century Club, where we talked about ethics, aesthetics, and insanity.

"Ken," I said, "I'm a man whose book has been destroyed. You won't print it without Liz's cuts and it won't sell as a White House handout. I could sue you now and you *know* I'd win: your case is laughable."

"Yes," he said, "I'm afraid you have a point."

"But then I'd lose my *book*; so I'm here to tell you that I want the book back: a clean release, no repayment of the advance. That's a small enough price for what's been done to me."

"Well, now . . ."

"Ken, you know damn well that Liz has no *right* in our editorial process. By the way, she sends her best and says you're a nut. She's just a bit overtrained in nut gathering too, I guess."

He tried to smile but failed. "Ralph, you *did* have her cooperation in doing the book."

"Which *doesn't* mean right of *approval*."

"You know, you're really making too much of all this; it happens in publishing all the time. Writers always have to make changes for editors."

"For editors, yes, but not for backward megalomaniacs. *She's* not my editor, *you* are, and you loved the book. You asked me to change four lines and I did. Ken, can't you *see*? This censorship is illegal and immoral and it also stinks. There's a *principle* involved and I swear I'll tell the whole story to the press. I have nothing to lose; I don't *care* what happens to me!"

"Ralph, you're sounding a little like Joan of Arc."

My own editor had now accused me of being a martyr in drag.

A few minutes later, he asked for another look at the manuscript, so I took him right to my home instead of waiting until Monday morning. As we rode uptown in a taxi, he had said, "Maybe we won't have to make *every* change she wants."

"*All* of them belong in *The Mikado*," I said. "Just making a few of them would ruin the book. I'm pretty sure I still want it back."

When we reached my apartment, I decided to make a last play for pity. While Judy talked to Ken in the living room, I went inside and brought out five-year-old Jill; and then I brought out Eve-Lynn, a toddling sixteen months; and finally, I presented the cat. I kept displaying living things that were dependent on me.

"I'll go over the whole manuscript tomorrow," said Ken as he left the Dickensian scene.

On Sunday afternoon, Dan called me. After carefully weighing all the factors involved except my career, he had decided that he couldn't let *anyone* print the book as I had written it because he wanted to keep the White House happy; and so, he now leaned towards a thoughtfully censored book at Doubleday, a children's book at Lippincott, or a picture spread in *Field & Stream*.

A few minutes later, I called Ken and said, "I've changed my mind. You can print the book in any form you want; just take my name off it. Why not use H. Allen Smith? I hear he has a future with you."

"I'm glad you've still got your sense of humor," he said. "And I'm glad you finally understand what's involved here. You see, Ralph, giving Liz a say is sort of an ethic beyond the contract. And you know, some of her changes aren't really that bad. For instance, I can see what she means when she says . . ."

For the next ten minutes, he defended the wisdom of the woman who had questioned his sanity. My own mind, however, was not on the voice of Nelson's Neville Chamberlain, but on a nearby newspaper photo of Lyndon Johnson, who was grinningly pointing to a big new scar across his hairy abdomen.

"You gotta present the President with *dignity*," Liz had said. Perhaps she had meant Woodrow Wilson.

On June 10, 1966, four months after the book had been officially killed by Doubleday, Him was officially killed too: run down by a government car in the White House driveway. If *only* the book had been out! I was sick to think of how many copies could have been sold at the funeral.

In early July, I learned from Stan Marks that Doubleday's flexible ethics had cost me thirty or forty thousand dollars. I responded by immersing myself in work instead of carbon monoxide: in new magazine pieces, the outline for a new book satirizing the great American tourist attractions, and the tale of my federal fiasco for *New York* magazine. Fiasco is fuel for a humorist and I had just been given a Texaco station bigger than any run by Feldman Oil.

By July of that year, I knew nothing could stop me, that writing was my compulsion, my hobby, my calling, my endless delight; and the money I got or lost had no effect on my love of the work. Dr. Johnson would have called me a blockhead, and I did qualify in other ways; but his thought about money as the primary reason for writing was no sounder than another Johnson's thought about beating the Vietcong with bombs.

Now, twenty years after I'd begun, I was still making notes at stoplights and after jumping from showers and in the middle of the night, when I patted the rug because my flashlight had rolled out of reach and I wanted to write down the latest lines that had come to me unbidden. I found myself insanely hating to have to go to sleep every night and waste seven hours before I could return to the current page, for I worked best in the morning, a time I kept expanding: I was now getting up as early as five, hoping that my typing and bumping into walls would not awaken the wife and two daughters who were in the shaky position of depending on me to keep the wolf away from the door. One hundred thousand sales of *Boy at the Fence*, of course, would have kept the wolf in Saskatchewan. Whether or not I was at my desk or my bed or my shower, the writing never stopped. Every time my eyes went glassy in a room full of people, when I forgot the name of the hostess or the town where I lived, Judy had to say, "Please excuse Ralph. He's writing." She knew how it felt to take the village idiot to tea.

At other times, I was writing to her: letters from the next room that I wrote in place of talk to present some idea because I thought better in print than in the bad first draft that was conversation.

"Honey, when you have a chance, read this," I would tell her, dropping a letter on the bed.

"Can't you just *tell* me what it says?" she'd reply. "It's a little crazy, you know, the way you play post office."

"*Please*—I *know* it's eccentric, but I've got it just right this way."

"Eccentric? You'd have to be a lot more normal to be called eccentric."

I knew I seemed ridiculous, but I was a helpless victim of a literary neurosis. My compulsion to always get all my language absolutely right, the relief and the sometimes exquisite pleasure such rightness kept giving me, applied not only to my work but to any words I put on paper. I was surely the only person in America who ever had done three drafts of a note to the United Parcel man.

Dan Kramer had taken back *Boy at the Fence* from Doubleday, which asked for no repayment of money, a gracious gesture for finks. All through the summer and fall, he'd been trying to place the book with another publisher, though it now seemed as enchanting as leg waxing to me.

"Anyway, it's dated," I said. "Him is dead."

"But *Johnson* is still alive," he replied.

"That's true. We'd really have a problem if Johnson had been run over instead of the dog."

Although I hadn't said it to Dan, I no longer cared if the book was published or left in the subway, for I had rebounded to other work. Judy had stopped teaching: Jill was six, Eve-Lynn was two, and they needed a full-time mother; so the challenge was mine, but I had a weakness for challenges and this one was irresistible. Supporting a family of four as a free-lance humorist was slightly harder than supporting them as a free-lance chimney sweep.

I was lucky, however, to be sustained by an exhilarating conceit, the conceit a writer needs in a world suggesting he get a job: that I could do things with words no one else could, that I had a unique voice, that I could work with originality in the manner of George Bernard Shaw, whose goal had always been with me:

"My method is to take the utmost trouble to find the right thing to say. And then say it with the utmost levity."

In a class at Columbia, Joseph Wood Krutch once memorably described the Shavian impact by telling me, "You never knew what Shaw was going to say; but once he said it, you'd think, *Of course: Shaw* would *say* that."

I knew I had wit, humor, and feeling, and a graceful way of blending the three. To counteract rejections by *The New Yorker* and the stockroom at Macy's, I savored the words of a writer at *New York* magazine: "You're as funny as Perelman, and you have heart."

Reading this tacky little burst of self-congratulation may move you to say, *Who cares? Who cares about* anything *you write?* At least once a week, I ask myself the same question and I'm happy I always know the answer: *Who cares?* is the one question a writer should never ask himself. The writer's business is usually pleasure: first, his own; and then, if he is lucky, the pleasure of whatever strangers he might engage. Noel Coward, whose work looks stronger to me each year and better than Arthur Miller's, summed himself up by saying, "I have a talent to amuse." It seems to me a writer cannot aim higher.

I never know how many strangers are enjoying or taking naps with my work, but I've always been able to please myself. I also know, however, what I *cannot* do. Because my talent for constructing a plot lies primarily in the consecutive numbering of pages, and because I prefer to invent satirical people rather than study real ones, traditional fiction is not my form. Any novels I write, like the one I did in 1974 called *Wasted on the Young*, must be flights of fancy, not slices of life. You go with your strength—and hope that the readers don't find it flab.

My strength has been printed humor—some personal, some satirical, and some unclassifiable—in both books and short pieces, like the many I did for *New York* from 1966 to 1970 with the encouragement of an imaginative editor named Clay Felker. It was Clay who let me look inside Manhattan's main post office to see why the mail could be delivered in rain and snow but not sunshine; and to look at the Army Induction Station that had processed me to see the remarkable medical breakthroughs in the presentations of new diseases; and to look at the competition for admissions to chic Manhattan nursery schools, a story in which I had the parents of a toddler saying:

"I *saw* her do well at Emanuel," said his wife, Vera, "but Dalton just whisked her away. If *only* she'd stopped sucking her thumb long enough to give at least *one* mature answer."

"I *told* you to paint that goddam thumb!" said Harry. "And what about . . ."

"I took her *twice* before the test."

"But the school wants the control to come from *her.* Vera, I *begged* you to cram her on that."

"We had to cram colors and *animals;* she's weak on elephants. Honey, we couldn't do *everything.*"

"Have you finished the application to Madison Avenue Presbyterian?"

"The questions are so *hard*—like this one: 'Was there anything special or unique about her way of learning to walk?'"

"We can't just say she put one foot in front of the other?"

"God, no: that's the sure road to City College. This thing is four pages, Harry, and the only easy question is: 'How long were you in labor?'"

"Hold on: that's a trick. We don't know if the school favors easy or hard deliveries. Do they want the child who took her time or the one who sprang right out of the gate?"

And it was Clay who pointed me towards jail.

ENTR'ACTE

In early 1968, I sold a fifteen-hundred-word piece to *Playboy*: a day in the lives of six presidential candidates done as a parody of a popular writer named Jim Bishop. In doing about eight drafts of the piece, first roughed out at more than two thousand words, I had kept cutting it down, following a basic principle of writing humor: Less is usually more. This principle does not mean that a fortune cookie is the pinnacle of comic prose. It means, upon deeper examination, that less is usually more.

A few days after *Playboy* had bought the piece, one of its editors called me and said, "Ralph, we'd like more."

"Fine," I replied. "I have an idea for one about—"

"No, more for *this* one. We want another three hundred words."

"But . . . the piece is *good* at this length."

"And it'll be even better when it's longer."

"No, it'll be even *worse*. I'll be spreading the material too thin and weaken the whole impact. It's the law of diminishing returns—really important in humor."

"How many credits am I getting for this course?"

"Dave, *you* know what I mean: in a funny piece, you have to leave 'em wanting more."

"Okay, so don't make the six candidates longer; just give us another one."

"Same problem: I'll start to repeat: it'll weaken the punch. Look at Lincoln at Gettysburg."

"Yeah, big laughs. All writers should get what Lincoln got."

"Well, you remember the old Sid Caesar show? Every sketch ran three or four minutes too long. They'd all have been better if they'd been shorter."

"Okay, I get the point. Now send us another three hundred words."

Because *Playboy* was a better market for humor than *Columbia College Today*, I now made the piece longer than it naturally wanted to be. Pretending that Shakespeare had said *Verbosity is the soul of wit*, I wrote three hundred words about another candidate, words that were a change of pace from the rest of the piece because they were less entertaining. They were, however, All-American words, for they were written in what S. J. Perelman had called "this country where size is all."

In mocking all the praise of Thomas Wolfe's overblown books, Thurber said, "The Genius is not supposed to labor over an idea until he cuts it down from 6,700 sprawling words to the three paragraphs which will express it perfectly, that is, bring it within the definition of Art."

You now may be asking: "Then why wouldn't your piece have been even better with *four* presidential candidates, or with *two*, or with just *one* who lost the nomination?"

The answer is that a piece of humor, like a pair of pants, should be neither too long nor too short, but just the right length. And how do you *know* what is just the right length?

That knowledge is part of your talent, just as a lawyer knows by instinct when to start his clock.

Here are two examples: first, what too much can do to humor; and then, what too little can do.

In April of 1974, I wrote for *New York* a parody of the purple salutes to nature that ran each Sunday as editorials in *The New York Times*. The shortest piece I ever wrote, this ironically is the only one that ever caused change: soon after it appeared, the valentines to vegetation stopped running. This effect, of course, was less impressive than the effect of *Das Kapital*, but it is probably easier to cause change in German.

APRIL

Coming as it does right after March and just before May, April is with us again, a thing of uncertain glory and five letters, each of which lifts up the heart and makes us giddy with the march of time. And if such giddiness moves us to spell things backwards, then let Lirpa arrive, rhyming as it does with Sherpa, who even in dreary Tibet senses April under his ice, pregnant with thirty-dayedness that makes its fans once more rejoice in post-equinox merriment.

Forget the first day, which is for fools, but bright and early on the second, long before the coming of the mail, April informs us that March is out of date and the trees we see and the checks we write have metamorphosed into something else. Now is the time that the scarlet tanager passes Orlando in that annual miracle, its trip up I-95. And now is the time that the robin and the CPA linger in their lofts at twilight as the days lust for summer, each a minute-thirty longer than the last. And we know from some lovely instinct lying deep within the race that summer will come at last and other seasons after that, just as our Neolithic ancestors knew it as the dawn of an age when no New England Mutual calendars covered the land. Like every bounty from the hand of Greenwich mean time, westward-wending April comes to the Fiji Islands first, but they need not cable us about it, for it's a charmer we have awaited, a beloved vernal vixen, now luring us like Mae West, now putting us off like Garbo. We yearn to hurry on to the roses and wine of May, but April says to tarry awhile and file our returns; and so, tarry we do, while the termites and meat prices rise and the voice of the poodle is heard in the land.

April is the burst of a cloud, the bloom of a bud, the name of a girl, one who knows that the Orioles and Cardinals are now on the wing, but it's Oakland eight-to-five.

Now note the damage of just a few phrases that do not belong in the comic mechanism.

APRIL, 1974

Coming as it does right after March and just before May, the month of April is with us again, and it certainly is a thing of uncertain glory and five letters, each of which lifts up the heart and makes us giddy with the march of time. And another thing: if such giddiness moves us to spell things backwards, as some dyslexics do, then let Lirpa arrive, rhyming as it does with Sherpa, who even in dreary Communist-controlled Tibet, senses April under his ice, pregnant with thirty-dayedness that makes its fans once more rejoice in post-equinox merriment and relaxation.

. Forget the first day, which is for fools, but bright and early on the second, long before the coming of the mail, whose delivery is a disgrace, April informs us that March is out of date and the trees we see and the checks we write have metamorphosed into something else. Now is the time that the really lovely scarlet tanager passes Orlando, in booming central Florida, in that annual miracle, its trip up I-95. And now is the time that the robin and the CPA linger in their lofts at twilight as the days lust for summer, each a minute-thirty longer than the last, for Galileo was right; check the almanac. And we know from some lovely instinct lying deep within the human race that summer will come at last and other seasons after that, just as our Neolithic ancestors also knew it as the dawn of an age when no New England Mutual calendars covered the land, or the dismal results of acid rain.

Like every bounty from the hand of Greenwich mean time, westward-wending April comes to the Fiji Islands first, but they need not cable us about it, for it's a charmer we have awaited, a beloved vernal vixen, now luring us like Mae West, now putting us off like Greta Garbo or another aloof star. We yearn to hurry on to the roses and wine of May, but April says to tarry awhile and file our tax returns; and so, tarry we do, while the termites and cost of living rise and the voice of the poodle is heard in the land.

April is the burst of a cloud, the bloom of a bud, the name of a girl, one who knows that the Orioles and Cardinals are now on the wing, but it's eight-to-five that the Oakland Athletics will win.

If you found any of the puffing up funny, it was funny only as satire of puffing up and not as part of the comic purity of the original piece. And if you think I'm starting to get lost in all this satirical overlapping, you're right. E. B. White did warn me.

However, even though I have only a B.A., I can't resist pointing out that the puffing up has destroyed one of the two basic functions of prose humor: the power of the art of the language itself when the words are comically right and exist for their own pure hilarity. The other function of humor, that ponderous business called revealing truth, is still working in the inflated version, though with less force. We still know that the man who writes those *Times* nature editorials is a schmuck, but we don't know it as entertainingly, so we don't know it as well. In fact, the puffing up may have elevated him to being only a jerk.

And speaking of jerks, let me now continue to ignore White's warning and show that humor *too* short can be as defective as too long. Just before "April" appeared, I had finally begun selling to *The New Yorker*, where one of the pieces I wrote contained these opening and closing sections:

Look for the Rusty Lining

My grandfather's hobby was worrying; and although hobbies are not usually considered inheritable, I am a talented worrier too. My grandfather's glum genes, which skipped my merry father, have flowered in me as major, all-purpose anxiety. A few weeks ago, for example, I learned that collapsing stars called black holes may soon suck up all the matter in the universe. Because I read this in *Vogue*, I hoped at first that the black holes were some kind of fad—a celestial pop event like Kohoutek or UFOs—but then I saw that the author of the article had been a visiting Member at the Institute for Advanced Studies in Princeton, and I knew that another crisis was at hand. Ominously, the Institute is just down the street from where I do *my* worrying.

The end of the universe should have been a splendid challenge for a gifted worrier like me, but mostly it upset me in a new and worrisome way, for it made me realize that I was spread too thin. When I found the black hole story, I hadn't nearly come to the end of an earlier wonderful worry about the polar ice cap melting and raising the level of the Atlantic Ocean enough to submerge the entire East Coast. I had been thinking of moving my family to Manitoba, but now that I was falling behind in my worrying, I had to worry if Manitoba might be tastier for a black hole than Princeton. On the other hand, Princeton was closer to those African killer bees that have been inexorably moving north from Brazil—the ones that made me decide to skip Guatemala Club Med this year.

In these terrible days, I often think of my grandfather, who was a nervous wreck in a simpler and happier time. His worries were transient and nicely manageable, such as: When would Mel Ott start hitting again? When would Connecticut run out of antiques? When would the Third Avenue El collapse? I miss him, but he is lucky not to be worrying today. I doubt he could have handled all the cosmic terrors; he might even have given up and become an optimist, thus losing the hobby he loved . . .

Actually, I've never had a worry as worrisome as the universe-destroying black holes because the universe is where I do all my worrying, and if it suddenly disappears, I may not be able to relocate. My only hope comes from a first principle of worry that I have learned from decades of anxiety: some of the biggest problems are half of a self-cancelling pair. A nice example is that dreaded polar ice cap, which some scientists say is *not* starting to melt but instead will begin to enlarge rapidly, causing a new ice age that soon will cover the entire United States.

I worried about this layer of ice from last May 17th until Labor Day, by which time my worry about the price of home heating oil had reduced it to the size of a rink. Lately, however, I have turned my mind back to the ice again, worrying that you cannot have ice that is growing and melting at the same time. One of these terrors is a dud, and the job of the dedicated worrier is to discover which one.

Applying this principle to the black holes, I wonder if there may not be some white holes in space as well: pretty, glowing things that won't digest a universe but may prefer to spit it back out. All I need is a new flash from the Institute about one of these, and then perhaps I will be able to start worrying about chinch bugs and the male menopause and all the other gentle terrors my grandfather could enjoy.

Is that the right way to spell "chinch bugs"?

Now see what just some slight misguided cutting can do to the rhythm and impact of the lines:

My grandfather's hobby was worrying, and mine too. A few weeks ago, for example, I learned that collapsing stars called black holes may soon suck up all the matter in the universe. I read this in *Vogue*, so I'd hoped the holes were some kind of fad, but then I saw that the author of the article had been a Member of the Institute for Advanced Studies in Princeton.

The end of the universe should have been a splendid challenge for a gifted worrier like me, but mostly it upset me because I was spread too thin. I still hadn't come to the end of an earlier worry about the polar ice cap melting and flooding the whole East Coast. I had been thinking of moving my family to Manitoba, but now I had to worry if that might be tastier for a black hole than Princeton. On the other hand, Princeton might be closer to those African killer bees, the ones that made me decide to skip Club Med this year.

There is no need to belabor the point by doing the same damage to the closing section. An editor with too lively a pencil and too tinny an ear might change the last line of the piece from *Is that the right way to spell "chinch bugs"?* to *Is that the right way to spell it?* thus ending it not with a bang but a whisper, a line he *also* might change to *Not with a bang but less.*

5

~

My Kind of Jail,
Chicago Has

Three years after my dark doings with Lyndon Johnson's dogs, I returned to the Secret Service by once more menacing the Republic with my subversive fancy. It was the summer of '68, a summer of discontent that made King Richard's winter seem like a month at Brighton Beach. In fact, in the whole grand sweep of American history, the three lowest moments are the construction of the first mall, the swearing in of Dan Quayle, and the 1968 Democratic National Convention, when the surrealism that had always engulfed me engulfed an entire city as well.

As a guest commentator for ABC News and a writer for *New York*, I went to Chicago that August to cover a convention that should have been covered only by Kafka, Curly, Larry, and Moe. On Monday, August 26, the convention's first night, I did a salute to Mayor Richard Daley, the last in a line of civic leaders going back to Hague, Crump, and Borgia. On the *ABC Evening News*, I said:

People are wondering why this convention is so festive, why there's a smile on the face of every National Guardsman and birdies are singing on the barbed wire fences . . .

A certain lunatic fringe of liberals, freethinkers, and Methodists says that Daley has suppressed freedom in Chicago by banning all outdoor meetings and parades. However, he *has* made the trains run on time . . .

About an hour after these words had gone out over the air, I was at the ABC studio in the convention hall, puckishly wearing the dark blue cap and pants of a convention usher for the magazine piece I was doing with photographer Jill Krementz. Suddenly, I was grabbed by a burly representative of the Chicago Police Department.

"Who the hell are *you*?" he inquired.

"I'm . . . Ralph Schoenstein," I unconvincingly replied.

"You an usher getting undressed or something?"

"No, I'm a writer."

"Jesus Christ, what a zoo. You happen to have any identification?"

While I nervously pulled out my press credentials, an ABC publicity man, Murray Gold, explained the reason for my strange outfit and then introduced Jill Krementz. When Murray had finished telling the premise of my story with both flair and force, the cop was no longer bewildered: he simply turned to me and said, "You're under arrest."

"Under *arrest*?" I said, disbelieving my life again. "What's the *charge*?"

"Impersonating a police officer," said the police officer.

Had I been impersonating a police officer, no talent agent would have touched me, for I was wearing a button-down shirt, a New York Mets tie clip, and I weighed 140 pounds, what the average Chicago cop bench pressed.

At this point, a captain arrived to help in the collaring of the undersized writer and the female photographer. He did a particularly thorough job of checking Jill's blouse for weapons.

"Tell this guy to keep his hands off me," she whispered as we were being led away.

"I'm not really in a position to give him advice," I said. "Maybe he's in love. Or maybe he's just a bit overtrained."

Fearful and incredulous, the two of us were taken to the Secret Service room and agents began to question us about our business in a city where young pacifists were threatening the general welfare, some of them attacking with folk songs. Suddenly, while I was wondering whether my military service counted for or against me, my psychic gears shifted from fear to the detachment that a writer sometimes feels while watching a scene from the ludicrous production that is his life. When one of the agents asked me if I ever had been a Communist, I thought again of the line, *Life is a dream, a little more coherent than most;* and then I wondered if I should reveal that at Stuyvesant High School I not only had been a United World Federalist, but I also had gone to a rally at the Astor Hotel for Henry Wallace—not because I loved the Progressive Party but because I loved Sandra Schwartz and dreamed of one day seeing if her nipples were as pink as her politics.

After the Secret Service had questioned us for about twenty minutes, Jill and I were made to wait in a corner of the room while checks were run on both of us. In this investigation, despite its generally nightmarish tone, I did have some luck: in 1968, no national network of police computers existed to tie me to Henry Wallace, Elizabeth Carpenter, or Louella Parsons.

At last, after more than an hour of checking, the Secret Service said that we were free to go; but Sergeant Radzicki of the Chicago Police Department had a dissenting opinion.

"She can go, but we want you," he said, directing me with an insistent hand on my starboard kidney.

"But I've been *cleared*," I told him.

"Not by us. Dressing up like a cop. You writers really are a bunch of wise little shits."

In the darkness outside a rear door of the convention hall, Radzicki shoved me into a patrol car that held a driver and a lieutenant, both of them also wearing blue helmets; and then off we rode into the night to have me booked on a charge of disorderly writing. Meanwhile, in nearby streets, members of the Youth International Party were being the conscience that Hubert Humphrey seemed to have lost as he tried to crawl towards the Presidency.

"Your first trip to Chicago, Mr. Bernstein?" said the lieutenant.

"No, I've been here before," I said. "I write for *Playboy.*"

"It figures. Porno guys covering politics now. You people are sick."

"I also write for *Today's Health.*"

"You wear funny costumes for them too?"

Just before midnight, we arrived at police headquarters on State Street, that great street. Radzicki got out first, opened the door for me, and asked the lieutenant, "Should I cuff 'im?"

I was delighted that mindless reality was giving me a better story than the one I had wanted to do with Jill involving no handcuffs. The lieutenant, however, allowed my hands to be free as he led me inside the old building and into an elevator that said FOR PRISONERS ONLY. At this moment, as the elevator door closed, I was struck by the realization that I was actually going to jail. An awareness of something like that in an elevator for prisoners in a police station is a writer's gift and it comes from deep within. You cannot learn it at the New School.

When I reached the desk sergeant on the ninth floor, Radzicki filled out an arrest form for impersonating an officer *and* criminal trespassing, while the sergeant said, "Take everything out of your pockets and put it up here. You can keep your wallet."

The cops were impassive as I took out my cash, keys, Kleenex, and Scripto; but when I added a gold tube of Max Factor Erace, the desk sergeant said, "Oh, terrific. A reporter *and* a fag."

"It's TV makeup," I told him, wondering if he ever watched anything besides Bugs Bunny. "Look, I'd like to call a lawyer."

"Right over there," he said, pointing to a phone on the wall near a row of cells.

My lawyer and literary agent, Arthur Hershkowitz, was asleep in New York, dreaming of the income of another of his clients, Jacqueline Susann; but I knew another lawyer who was at the convention, Jerry Ruddy, although his defense of me might have lacked something because he wasn't licensed to practice in Illinois. His specialty, however, was theatrical law, so he was ideal for the charge of impersonating an officer.

"Ralph, you weren't the only writer arrested tonight," said Jerry from the convention hall. "They got Murray Kempton too. They're going insane."

"And I may join them," I said, hoping that I might be able to share a cell with Murray Kempton instead of with some right-wing pimp. "Jerry, it's not just the ridiculous impersonation charge: they're *also* charging me with criminal trespassing—in my *own studio!* It's like Nuremberg with these guys!"

"Watch that kind of talk: they'll think Nuremberg is something bad. Okay, just sit tight."

"I think I'll be able to do that."

"I'll be right down and see if I can get you out."

Back at the desk sergeant's post, after I had signed a receipt for my money, pencil, and keys, another cop searched me with pats that made me think of the way I put powder on my daughters after a bath. And then, just as I was wondering if my police record might keep Jill and Eve-Lynn out of Dalton, Tom Hayden was brought in. One of the leaders of the group called Yippies, he had a cleanly shaven face, a fresh white shirt, and pressed khaki pants, an appearance that moved Radzicki to tell me, "Here comes another animal."

"No, he's a damn good man," I said, as Hayden emptied his pockets only a few feet from me.

"Why the hell don't he stay home where he belongs?"

"Because he happens to be fighting for the country's soul."

"Now *who* told you crap like that? These stupid kids, it's just a big party."

"Do *you* go to a party to have your head cracked open?" I said; but I was making no impression on Radzicki's own well-insulated head. Turning to Hayden, I was about to introduce myself when Radzicki said, "Okay, Mister Mouth, fin-gerprints."

A few minutes later, while I was washing off the ink but sa-voring the memory of having my fingerprints taken, about ten more Yippies were brought in, some of them better dressed than I had been when asked not to lower the tone of my apartment house. Silently, these party animals walked to the desk and emptied their pockets. One of them was holding a handkerchief on the back of a skull that some arm of the law undoubtedly had tried to ventilate.

"Look at 'em: all on LSD," said Radzicki, whose own mental condition could not have been blamed on drugs.

And now I found myself walking away from him to stand near the Yippies, proud to have been booked with them and sorry that my own charge involved not a noble cause but a bit of burlesque. I also regretted having just moments with them be-fore they were taken to a cell and I was taken for a class picture.

Once again, as I had done at my fingerprinting, I was living a boyhood radio show, not one of Norman Corwin's but *Mister District Attorney*. I was supposed to have *been* Mister District Attorney and here I was posing for a post office wall. Thinking sadly of what my late grandfather would have said about my mug shot, even though Lepke *was* Jewish, I took my place be-fore a mounted Polaroid camera and then a cop hung a board around my neck that carried the date and a number.

"You better take off your glasses," he said.

"But without my glasses," I said, "it isn't me. You'll just be making it tough for yourselves to grab me again."

"I still like you better with 'em off," he said, being as creative as my charges.

After taking a full face shot, he waited for the image to appear and then showed it to me. Delighted by my appearance because it didn't look like me, I said, "Any chance I could get a copy of that?" Judy didn't have a decent prison picture of me.

"Now *you* know I couldn't do that. What are you in for anyway?"

"Disorderly writing."

"Sure, I knew you wasn't one o' *them.*" He looked toward where the Yippies had started to sing "We Shall Overcome."

"Goddam animals."

When the photographer had taken a profile shot, another cop came and led me back toward the cells, for my preadmission work was over and it was time to become a resident in what *Newsweek* recently had called "the worst jail in America." The cop took me not to the Yippies but to an empty block; and there he opened one cell door, I walked in, he closed and locked it, and Cook County began correcting me.

The lack of freedom in jail was surely a problem, but I quickly discovered another: there was nothing to do. Squelching a moment of panic caused by having no pencil, newspapers, or books, I sat down on one of the bunks and tried to lose myself in reading my wallet. My driver's license, however, lacked a certain compelling sweep, so I marked my place in the wallet and began to pace around the cell.

The decor of the cell was early Industrial Revolution: the understated appointments were two wooden bunks without mattresses, one filthy sink, and a toilet bowl for which a seat was considered a luxury. But at last, I did find something to read: a wall with some political analysis, part of which said:

2, 4, 6, 8,
CHICAGO IS A POLICE STATE

Had I a pencil, I would have enriched the anthology with:

NO VERSE MAKES THIS CELL LESS CRUDDY.
WHERE THE HELL IS JERRY RUDDY?

Near the couplet about Chicago was a half-finished game of boxes that gave me a pang, for this was the game I had often played with Jill. Turning away from the boxes to try to turn off thoughts of home, I thought instead about writers who had gone to jail: Dostoyevsky, Thoreau, and Wilde. No matter how grim the imprisonment, none of them had been made to leave his pencil at the desk, a pencil I desperately needed now: ideas were coming to me and I was going mad with the frustration of being unable to write them down. I was a compulsive note-maker: I made them on napkins, envelopes, and the backs of blank checks; and once, driving paperless on the New Jersey Turnpike, I had written some lines in ink in the blank spaces of a toll ticket and then transferred them to a napkin at a Roy Rogers, where I had asked the manager, "Do you happen to have any whiteout? I'd like to erase my Turnpike ticket." She had smiled, but her eyes seemed to say, *Please—go blow up Burger King instead.*

And now, in Chicago, I didn't even have a pen. Suddenly, however, I saw that I still had my tie clip and I found I could use the squared edge of it to make impressions on a piece of blank paper that had been in the pocket of my jacket. While I was copying a couplet from the wall that had tried, à la Emily Dickinson, to rhyme "Humphrey backer" with "motherfucker," a cop came to my cell, opened it, and led me to a screen door. On the other side, in all his illicit splendor, was Jerry Ruddy.

"Jerry, these charges are *nonsense*," I said.

"*You* know that and *I* know that," he said, "but *they*—look, for some reason, your case has gone all the way up to Daley."

"You mean all the way *down* to Daley."

"Now don't make any more trouble than we already have. I'm really not supposed to practice in this state, you know."

"That thought has been comforting me all night."

"The problem is I can't get you out until your fingerprints clear the FBI. Just sit tight."

And so, feeling tired, hungry, dirty, and depressed, I returned to the ideal place to sit tight, wondering if the FBI would consider me a vagrant because I hadn't held a job for eleven years. Would it count in my favor that my father worked for Hearst and every year staged I Am An American Day? Would it count against me that my grandfather felt the only real Americans were Jews?

At last, trying to forget Richard Daley, the FBI, and Jerry's bar exam, I lay down on some wooden slats, put my folded jacket under my head, and closed my eyes; but the overhead fluorescent light came pouring through my lids, so I put my right forearm over my face and tried to relax.

Puff, the magic dragon,
Lived by the sea,

My lullaby was a song by the Yippies that I'd often enjoyed with my daughters while watching Captain Kangaroo, and I found myself singing along:

And frolicked in the autumn mist
In a land called Honalee.

"Hey, why are *you* singing that stuff?" said a passing cop. "You're not one of them."

Deciding not to confuse him with my love of Captain Kangaroo, a man he might have thought was a precinct commander, I said, "Listen, doesn't this place have any *mattresses?*"

"You know what they'd do with *mattresses* in here?"

"Sleep on 'em?"

"No, tear 'em up and stuff 'em down their throats."

I understood this observation as well as I understood everything else that had happened to me this night; but I was saved from self-pity by perspective: in a world where American men were being killed in an Asian civil war while American children were being killed by rampaging viruses and speeding drunks, the brief incarceration of a writer craving a mattress and a malted milk simply had no place in the general woe.

The Marxist melody makers were softly singing "Blowin' in the Wind" when I finally fell into a sleep that was understandably dreamless, for all the dreams had been coming while I was awake.

I knew that my nap ended precisely at 5:08 because of the watch I now realized I could have been playing with: I could have turned it ahead seven hours and pretended that I was in the Bastille, a slightly better prison than this one, for I had been here since midnight without a mattress, a charge that made sense, or a mention of food.

About twenty minutes later, the cell door opened again and I was led down a long hallway and into a courtroom, where Jerry was standing before a judge. As I took my place beside him, he whispered, "It's all taken care of; I had to spread some ABC money around. Just say you're sorry and pretend you're coming back for trial."

"*Trial?*" I said. "But the charges are so—"

"Look, Patrick Henry, it's a *fix.*"

"Really?"

"Yeah, one nice thing about this Daley gang: they may drag you here for no reason, but you can buy your way right out. So just apologize to this guy after he tells you you're a schmuck."

More elegantly than Jerry, the judge then told me what I was for having put on a blue uniform at the convention; and I responded with a movingly repetitious apology, for apologizing was a talent of mine. In fact, when I'd been in nursery school, my teacher had told my mother, "For some reason, Ralph likes to say 'I'm sorry.' He really belongs at a school in Japan."

My latest apology contained a promise to never again impersonate a Chicago policeman, a restriction I felt I could live with; but then, instead of dismissing me cleanly, the judge said, "Return for trial September seventeenth."

"You staying for the second night of the convention?" said Jerry in the elevator taking me to freedom.

"No," I said, "I think I'll go home and concentrate on playing boxes."

Moments later, I walked out into the predawn darkness of Chicago. Chicago, City of the Big Shoulders. Chicago, that toddlin' town. Chicago, where I had spent more time in jail than Al Capone.

On the morning of September eighteenth, I was at home writing a piece on how to put children to sleep, hoping that one way wouldn't be to read the piece to them, when the telephone rang and I heard my mother's voice:

"Ralph, look at page ten of *The Times*! There's a warrant for your *arrest* in Chicago!"

"Jesus," I said, "you sure it's *me?*"

"The headline says WARRANT FOR HUMORIST and the story has your name."

"Does it mention any of my books?"

"You were supposed to be there yesterday for a *trial*. How could you *forget* a thing like that?"

Although my stomach was sinking, I kept a light tone for my mother.

"Mom, I can't be expected to remember *everything*. Look, I'm sure it's just a misunderstanding. Let me get off now and make a call."

"Well, let me know if you're going back to jail because I'd like to have all of you over for Rosh Hashanah."

Five minutes later, Jerry told me what had happened: the Chicago court clerk had kept ABC's bribe and then decided that I also should come to trial. What poor form! If you're going to be crooked, play *fair*: don't take a bribe and administer justice *too*.

Feeling more frightened than I had been at any time during my night in Chicago, I took a crash course in extradition and learned it was done for only high crimes. Nevertheless, I was now an outlaw in Chicago, the shaky launching pad for my first book. Precisely eight years before, on September 18, 1960, after three days of radio and television promotion for *The Block*, I had found that no *Blocks* were in Chicago: the Random House shipment had never arrived. Two weeks later, the shipment still hadn't arrived, and I had stopped checking.

And now, with a smile for Mrs. O'Leary's cow, I went back to work, aware that for the first and only time in my life, I was America's most wanted writer.

ENTR'ACTE

An early twentieth-century Spanish columnist named Julio Camba once said that he could write a funny piece about anything, but he was talking through his sombrero: he could not have dipped with comic success into the *Lampoon's* compost heap and he also could not have written a funny piece about something that already satirized itself, a subject so surrealistic that no wit, no matter how inventive, could ever enrich it.

Camba was unlucky to have lived before Excedrin, but he was lucky to have written before *Donahue,* before an age in which the bizarre has become so commonplace that the satirist turns away in despair because embellishment is impossible. One afternoon on national television, I heard Phil Donahue ask a young woman, "So your husband left you and married your mother?"

How do you embellish *that?* How do you launch *that* into comic flight? Your only chance might be to lift it into verse:

> *So your husband's major flaw*
> *Was to marry his mother-in-law?*

Even such rhyme, however, would have had more punch in the age of Gilbert and Sullivan, before farce had come down from the stage and into our living rooms. Too many talk show subjects defy satirical development: on just one day near Thanksgiving of 1989, three of the shows fearlessly explored these compelling American issues: Nurses Who Murder Their

Patients, Phoenix Cross-Dressers Over Sixty, and Women Who Are Married to Jerks.

Were some of those women married to men who still believed in taste?

Reality has always contained enough of the ridiculous so we could say "Truth is stranger than fiction." Nevertheless, there was a time, from 560 B.C. to 1985, when surrealism was not the norm with which the humorist had to compete. In 1931, for *Of Thee I Sing*, George S. Kaufman and the Gershwins created a satirical Vice President of the United States named Alexander Throttlebottom; but even these brilliant men could not have spoofed the Vice Presidency today because life has trumped art with a parody named Dan Quayle.

Although I should have learned long ago that I cannot launch a comic flight from something that already is in orbit, I still couldn't resist trying to take off on a newspaper story that ran in March of 1989:

> TOKYO (AP) Japan's chief government spokesman yesterday defended Prime Minister Noburu Takeshita's statement that it is difficult to judge whether Japan was an aggressor in World War II. Takeshita has said that some people believe the war began by accident or was fought in self-defense. He said the question of whether Japan was an aggressor would have to be decided by historians in the future.

In full satirical salivation, I grabbed a legal pad and wrote:

> Now that the passage of time has allowed us to gain some perspective, it is possible to see at last who was really involved in World War II, if that's what you want to call it, and how the whole thing came out. The Japanese *may* have been involved, of course—there was a lot of smoke and confusion that first day—but if Japanese involvement *is* finally proven

And then I hit the only kind of writer's block I've ever known: the one that blocks me when I'm dumb enough to try to top one of life's own ludicrous absolutes. A Japanese Prime Minister who is uncertain about whether Japan was an aggressor in World War II is a man who belongs in *The Mikado*, singing:

> *Here's a how-de-do.*
> *Who started World War Two?*
> *Was it nine Brazilian bombers*
> *Manned by cocky coffee farmers*
> *Or one Danish crew,*
> *Maybe sniffing glue?*

6

~

Droppings in the Arena

Eight years after Jerry's wallet had helped me pay my debt to society, I wrote my eighth book, *Yes, My Darling Daughters*, a work that moved my Aunt Ida to say, "Have you read the new Michener? If you can just get through the first two hundred pages, it's really great."

I had wanted to reply, *If you can just get through the first two hundred pages of* Yes, My Darling Daughters, *you're forty pages past the end.*

In happy contrast to Aunt Ida's devout indifference to my new book, *Kirkus Reviews* generously called me "undisputed king of the genre." I knew, however, that if indeed I was reigning over the genre of fathering, my kingdom was still too small for all the earnest American book buyers who now liked their literature by the pound. I knew that if Hemingway had written *The Old Man and the Sea* in 1976, he would have had to begin it with a brief history of Havana, or at least a solid essay on how to clean tuna.

Because of my inability to ever move my books out the *front* door of Macy's, my mother from time to time had told me, "Why don't you start writing for television?" her tender way of saying, "Why don't you start writing for money?" But I always had found so much pleasure in writing prose that I had never wanted to leave it for one of the life-supporting arts. Moreover, Joseph Wood Krutch had said, "Of all the instruments ever invented for communicating an artist's vision, the printed word is still the most versatile." Of course, had his agent been able to line up a sitcom on scorpions for him, Krutch might not have spoken these words to which I clung so grandly.

Although my love of prose was genuine, I did take occasional detours, and every one of them was a dead end. For example, just before the publication of *Yes, My Darling Daughters*, a Broadway producer named Lorin Price asked me to write the book for a musical version of *The Hunchback of Notre Dame*. For sheer rottenness, this idea could have been topped only by a musical comedy of the Torah, or perhaps by a musical of *Pilgrim's Progress* called *Step Right Up!* Nevertheless, unable to resist such a splendidly moronic challenge, I accepted Price's offer and worked for more than two months to move *The Hunchback of Notre Dame* from the page to the stage, trying all the while to keep myself from thinking about such natural songs for the show as "If I Were a Bell" and "I've Grown Accustomed to His Face."

At last, however, I was defeated by the job, especially by the scene in which the most believable character is a goat, and I returned to the world of prose, aware that *The Hunchback of Notre Dame* might have been convertible to a musical, but only by a writer who could stop laughing at it. The best work that I had done on the show was not a dramatization of any scene but a prediction of a line from one of the reviews:

At the end of this show, we are left to think about the score, which is a tie:
Notre Dame—nothing
Audience—nothing

Not long after I had tried to make my Broadway gargoyle, I embarked on another detour; for, contrary to what Darwin had thought about the difference between me and a chimpanzee, I seemed to lack the ability to predict predictable mistakes; and so, when CBS took an option on *Yes, My Darling Daughters* and offered me the chance to write a pilot script, I accepted as if I knew how to do it.

On a Monday morning in November of 1976, I elatedly entered the New York office of Bernard Bach, the CBS Vice President for Eastern Program Development. There I met Bach, a man in his fifties, and three of his assistant developers: Harvey Cream, a man in his forties; Marty Mayflower, a man in his thirties; and Sally Wren, a woman in her twenties. What bound them all together was a desperation to please people in their preteens.

"What *numbers* Freddie got with *Laverne* last night," said Mayflower after I had been introduced. I was hearing envy of Fred Silverman, the programming whiz at ABC, spoken by a man whose network now was behind both ABC and NBC, and possibly ham radio too.

"Yeah, *Laverne* is what they want," said Cream. "Schlemiel, Schlimazel, Hassinfeffer Incorporated."

After a few more minutes of talk about how many minds had been captured by *Laverne and Shirley*, a meeting began to see if these modest minds would also surrender to *Yes, My Darling Daughters.*

"Ralph, your book is hilarious and touching," said Bach, "and the demographics for hilarious and touching are usually strong, especially around the holidays; but the only problem is . . . well, I just don't know if families are 'in' right now."

"But haven't they really been 'in' for the last few thousand years?" I replied. "I mean, unless something big happened over the weekend that—"

"No, what I mean is funny-touching *reality*-type programs. We may not be in that cycle right now."

It sounded as though he was talking about a washing machine.

"But ABC is doing a pilot of *Eight Is Enough*," I said, seeing my reality-type daughters missing their chance to be household words.

"Yes, we know Freddie's doing that," said Cream, "but will it *go*? We've got to wait for the numbers."

"And you're short six kids," said Mayflower with a grin that made me want to suture his lips.

"I'm having *more!*" I said in a burst of fertility and greed. "My wife is pregnant right *now*." I stopped short of offering to bring a note from Judy's obstetrician.

In spite of the fears that came so naturally to these four television pioneers, they finally agreed that my inadequate number of daughters did have a chance to capture millions of American minds; and now they began to tell me all the pretested universals that I should weave into the script for which I'd be paid thirteen thousand dollars, the amount I would have earned for five hundred twenty "Doubletakes" had the *Journal-American* still been alive.

"The next thing we want to do is show you what *not* to do," said Bach. "Marty, take Ralph in and show him that Gelbart pilot so he can avoid all those mistakes."

Another lesson in how not to write would have been *Ball Four*, the only show the eastern programmers had produced that year: it resembled a high school play, though slightly less professional. Of the more than two hundred shows that the eastern wing had in development, only six had become pilots and only this one had reached the air. None of the others could have been worse, for *Ball Four* was a shining absolute. The others, however, had *tested* worse: they had not been sufficiently appreciated by the select groups of shoppers, tourists, truants, and drifters who had been lured from the street by CBS to apply their aesthetic sensibilities to television art.

"This Gelbart thing seemed to have all the right elements," said Mayflower as we took seats in the screening room; and there I saw a twenty-four-minute comedy whose story was trite, whose characters were clichés, and whose jokes were predictable. The photography was excellent.

When the screening was over, my creative mission was clear. After saying good-bye to the committee, I walked out of the CBS building and stopped at the corner for a red light. Suddenly, a long-haired young man in a leather jacket emerged from a doorway and approached me with a smile. I was expecting him to ask if I was interested in his sister or a diamond ring for thirty bucks, but instead he said, "Wanna test a new TV show?" And then he gave me a card that invited me back into the building at three o'clock to help doom the work of a writer like me.

The following morning, I began to write my first television script, uneasy about abandoning the appealing permanence of print; but I also remembered what Somerset Maugham had said when he abandoned books for plays: he would never have to describe another sunset.

I was not, however, a describer of sunsets, or even early afternoons. Moreover, instead of losing the oppressiveness of nature by leaving prose, I was losing my voice, the thing that makes a writer unique, the thing that distinguishes him from the author of a driving manual. I was probably not the first writer to realize that a play was all dialogue; but the more I worked on turning one chapter of my book into a play, the more I felt I was writing with one hand tied behind my back; and that hand, to mix an anatomical metaphor, was my voice. A playwright never can comment on the action he presents unless he talks to someone in the back of the theater.

A good example of what can be lost in moving from the page to the stage is to move these immortal lines of Ring Lardner's *The Young Immigrunts:*

Are you lost daddy I arsked tenderly.
Shut up he explained.

In turning this prose dialogue into the oral, we could survive the loss of "I arsked tenderly," though it does help to set things up. But how could we survive the loss of the sublimely funny "he explained"? The comic explosion seems to be missing in:

SON: Are you lost, Daddy?
FATHER: Shut up.

It was painful for me to turn my own work into a television script because, as seen in the death of this Lardner exchange, dialogue in prose is just one dimension of the work: the other is the writer's third-person voice, as heard in this passage from my book:

My devout little daughter was pushing for Chanukah, with its sacred giving of eight gifts, while her father once again was about to let his heart be melted by packaged Christianity. However, on December 6th, I guiltily took a grab at Chanukah by stopping at a synagogue and saying to a woman who worked there, "I'd like a dreidel for the first night of Chanukah. I'm tired of my daughters playing poker at this holy time."

"The first night of Chanukah was Monday," she replied. "This is the fourth."

As I left the synagogue, wondering if Jews did anything special on Pearl Harbor Day, I knew that the girls and I were truly the lost tribe of Israel. All through that holiday season, our merry seven-card stud went on, with deuces, one-eyed jacks, and red fives wild. Even pagan purity eluded us.

Not only did I feel pain from turning such lines into pure dialogue, but I was also being encouraged by the network to write down, and down was not an appealing direction. By the mid-seventies, I was a much better writer than I had been when I wrote *The Block* and I wanted to keep growing. *The Block* was the best I had been able to do at twenty-six and it was good work; but the only writing that should be the same at twenty-six and forty-three is your signature.

I brooded about these matters all during the writing of the script; and when I had finished, true to my new medium, I tested it: on a random wife, who happened to be the first reader for everything I wrote. Blessed with high intelligence, superb taste, and an excellent ear for language, Judy read all of my penultimate drafts and then made comments that moved me either to thank her or move to a motel. I wanted her always to be honest within the context of always loving everything I wrote; and while she was loving with honesty, I wanted her to feel no pressure.

Judy was my biggest fan; she once told me she had fallen in love with me while reading *But I Always Called Them Sir;* but she was also my toughest critic and her readings of my drafts were good tests of our marriage.

"This is nice," she would say after reading a new piece.

"That's *all?*" I'd reply. "Nice? A *pot* roast is nice."

"That's it: I'm not reading another one. From now on, you can show your stuff to the mailman. He's an easy laughter."

"Hey, I'm sorry; I just meant . . ."

"You just meant: Come, let us adore him. I *like* it, but there are things I've liked more. And now you're going to sulk for two days like the professional you are."

"No, no, let me have your notes. I'll really consider all the changes, I promise. You *know* I always do; you always catch things. It's just that . . . well, I'm hung up on knocking you out with everything I write. Too hung up, I guess. Your opinion is so important to me."

"Joyce Carol Oates never shows a *thing* to her husband because she doesn't want to take a chance on hurting the marriage."

"*I* wouldn't show my stuff to her husband either; but you *know* I write everything for you."

"And *you* know I think most of your things are wonderful. Except the fighting about how wonderful they are."

"Honey, didn't this one make you laugh out loud anywhere?"

"When will you finally learn that I never laugh out loud at what I read?"

I had married Judy in spite of this character flaw: she is an internal laugher, not a pretty sight; and because of this flaw, I sometimes am stupidly jealous of playwrights and screenwriters able to cause audible laughter with second-rate work. All I can do when feeling so childish is remember what Moss Hart said in *Act One:*

> . . . One participates not only in the play but also in the reactions of the audience. One senses as one never can while reading a book that one is sharing an experience . . . Everyone who has ever both seen and read a comedy knows that something which can at best provoke a smile when met on the printed page may be irresistibly hilarious when shared with an audience.

In spite of the quieter audience, I would always prefer the permanence and three-dimensionality of a book to a play. However, I was now in Moss Hart's world with my television script; and when Judy read it, though she did have questions about certain words and a reminder that this was for the ear and not the eye, she was rhapsodic, either because she had loved it or because she was not in the mood for a fight.

With high spirits, I sent the script to Bernie Bach and then spent ten anxious days until he called. During that time, I played the piano a lot, for my playing relaxed me, though it seemed to have a different effect on everyone else.

"We love it," Bernie finally said, "and we want to see you right away. We have some notes for you."

I felt a little chill. I never minded notes from Judy or a wise book editor; but in broadcasting, the only notes I wanted were good E-flat harmonies.

*   *   *

When I walked into Bernie's office for the meeting, I found Harvey, Marty, Sally, and a new man who had "just come in from the Coast" and whose name was either Bud Cherry or Cherry Bud; I wasn't paying attention to names because I was listening to Marty and Harvey worshiping Fred Silverman.

"Did you see the *numbers* Freddie got with *Kotter* last night?" said Marty.

"They were *numbers*," said Harvey, shrewdly aware that they weren't letters.

These two men spent more time looking back at Silverman than ahead to their own new works, possibly because their own new works would *be* Silverman's old ones.

"Ralph, we love the script," said Bernie, "but we have a few notes for small revisions that we'd like you to think about."

"Tell me," said Bud Cherry, "why does the father go out of the house to see the neighbor at the start of the second act?"

"Because his lawn mower is broken and he wants to borrow one," I said, revealing my piercing insight into the human heart.

"But *why* does he need a mower just then?" said Bud.

"He wants to cut the grass." My understanding of mankind was nothing short of Shakespearean.

"And the mother. Is she really likeable enough?"

"Well . . . yes. The *father* likes her. And so do the girls."

"I'm just wondering if they're going to accept her."

"Who, the family?"

"No, the viewers. Of course, it does depend on whether we're aiming for early or late in the evening. If she's an eight o'clock mother, I'm not sure she should be quite so ironic."

"But that's character definition; these people aren't a Brownie troop. I mean, I'm not writing *The Brady Bunch*."

What a baroquely idiotic remark I had just made. Cherry would have traded all the character definition in *Macbeth* for *The Brady Bunch*, which was now in reruns in Guam.

The rest of the meeting was a critical smorgasbord in which I was given a chance to choose from constructive opinions that cancelled each other out.

"I think you should strengthen the mother," said Bernie.

"But keep her more in the background," said Sally.

And on my legal pad, I wrote: *Stronger but weaker mom.*

When the meeting was over and my pad was rich with Zen ideas, I knew that Bernie had been right: the committee did love my script. All they wanted changed were the words.

Rewriting when you have no idea what you're doing takes a little longer than rewriting with a plan in your head, so I needed almost a month to do my new script. As I rewrote and unwrote and nonwrote, yearning to return to the one-to-one relationships of publishing, I kept wondering which members of the committee I should be trying to please. At last, in a flash of acumen, I decided to please the ones who might still be there when I turned in the script. Because my agent, Artie Hershkowitz, had told me that Marty Mayflower was about to be fired, I ignored Marty's suggestion to make the father a bus inspector instead of a writer; and, just for fun, I also ignored Harvey's suggestion to make one of the children an adopted refugee from Haiti.

The script that I finally sent back to the committee was half as good as my original; and therefore, it had twice the chance to get on the air.

Almost two weeks later, Bernie called to invite me to "take another meeting" the following Thursday, undoubtedly to see what could be done about the originality still left in the script. When Thursday came and I walked into Bernie's office, I found that Marty indeed was gone and his place had been taken by a new man whose name and coast I missed because I was concentrating on memorizing a defense of my script.

Eve-Lynn says line three on page ten, I would tell Bud today, *because those are the words that come into her head. It's an offbeat technique sometimes used by Tennessee Williams*

I was also ready to loudly remind my collaborators that, while we were dismantling my script and wondering if families were in or out, *Eight Is Enough* had gone on the air at ABC and become another hit to be copied over here. Would we now drop *Welcome Back, Kotter* as a model and use *Eight Is Enough?* Or would our inspiration now be *Cheaper By the Dozen?*

As the meeting began, I was still rehearsing my defense of my daughters' dialogue when Bud suddenly said, "Ralph, there's just one problem that's bothering me. I'm afraid I don't like the arena."

"The arena?" I said, wondering what the hell he was talking about, for my story took place not in the Astrodome but a suburban house.

"Yes, the family arena. It may be wrong."

"But it's the heart of my *book.* I mean, that's what it's *about.*"

"Maybe, but it still can be fixed. Any reason we can't take the story out of the house?"

"Because they don't *live* out of the house. And this particular story is about their *selling* the house."

"Why don't we just lose the parents and follow the kids?" said Harvey.

"You mean . . . like *Kotter?*" I said.

"Right: put the show in a *school.*"

"Why not?" said Sally.

I felt like a Western settler encircled by backward Indians. "But . . . you want the *kids* . . . to sell the *house* . . . from the *school?*"

"Well, maybe not precisely *that,*" said Harvey, "but let's not rule anything out. There's always a way to lick everything."

Especially me, I thought.

By the end of the meeting, I knew I no longer could fight the forces of Oz. My story about the comic struggles of a writer and his family to sell their home had become the story of two teenagers at an all-girl public high school.

"It's terrific and it's *new,*" said Bud. "*Kotter* accents the boys and that leaves a whole sex free for us: we'll be punching up the *girls.*"

"Just one problem," said Harvey. "Teenage boys would rather watch girls, but teenage *girls* would rather watch *boys*. The demographics are pretty clear."

"Okay, put both sexes in," Bernie told me, "so we'll be nicely covered."

"At an all-girl high school?" I said, suddenly nostalgic for the creative delights of *The Hunchback of Notre Dame* and *Boy at the Fence.*

"It smells like a hit," said Bud.

With a different scent in mind, I returned to my desk and called Artie Hershkowitz to report the redirection of the script toward Munchkinland.

"They want to put the whole thing in an all-girl *public* high school?" he said. "There *aren't* any. In fact, they're illegal: every public school has to be coed."

At once, I called Harvey and said, "There's a problem with our new arena: it doesn't exist. There *are* no all-girl public high schools in the United States."

"I'd like to see the demographics on how many people know that," he said.

"Harvey, I don't care if only one hermaphrodite in *Idaho* knows it. I just can't fake a premise like that."

"But there's such a thing as poetic license."

"You want me to take poetic license in *addition* to lying? The only way we could keep this premise would be to put the story back in the fifties, like *Happy Days.*"

"Well, maybe you should think about something a little closer to *Happy Days.* Then you could bring back the mother and father."

"Harvey, what I'm going to be bringing back is my *dinner:* I've got a nervous stomach from working like this and I just can't keep doing it. I can't keep writing a collection of options."

"Okay, I hear you; we'll freeze it. Just sort of fudge the kind of school it is and then we'll see how to play it when we test."

Moments after I had hung up in disbelief and despair, I was struck by a terrifying vision of the spread of pretested art, the spread of creation by general election, beyond the swamp of TV. I saw the director of the New York City Ballet stopping people at Lincoln Center to ask, "Would you rather see lifts or leaps? Do you favor reducing the size of the tights so you could see a little more flesh? Would you like to see an occasional hamstring pulled? And would you rather see ducks than swans?"

Rudderless, I began to write the story of two fetching teenage girls who were best friends at an all-neuter high school; and I kept trying to move them out of the school to avoid having to show other students because I couldn't figure out what sex they were.

"Maybe you should have the whole thing take place during an epidemic of typhoid," said Judy one night while I was taking Pepto Bismol before another study of humor on ABC. "Then you could just show the two of them alone in quarantine."

"I like it," I said, "and quarantine is a lovely arena; but I don't know how typhoid would test. Now *dysentery* maybe . . . I had it in the Army and I think I have it again."

I was studying ABC's comedies because I was now a writer moved not by visions from within but cartoons from without. I was a writer who had been working for more than two months on a twenty-five-minute play in which the two leads had just become the stars of a basketball team at a high school in the twilight zone. However, this newest metamorphosis of the girls, while clearly demographic dynamite, did give me some concern: although putting the girls in a varsity sport would be reflecting a major school trend, the shows on CBS were designed to reflect not life but ABC, and ABC had no show about varsity females that was available for imitation.

When I had finished my latest revision of a story that no doubt would evolve into a tale of the Brontë sisters, I sent it to Bernie; and this time he responded in less than three weeks.

"It's wonderful, Ralph," he said. "Come right in for some notes."

And "notes" was the proper word, for the following day in his office, I found that another programmer had hopped on the merry-go-round: in the room was a new man, whose name I didn't want to know. The new man from our previous meeting, whose name I almost knew, was also there; so I was now collaborating with two strangers and three friends I didn't like.

"This is generally fantastic," said Bud, "except for one thing: you haven't made the girls ethnic enough. Protestants don't work in a sitcom; they're too bland."

"Ralph, *are* they Protestants?" said Harvey, turning Torquemada.

"Well, gee . . . I'm afraid I don't *know*," I said. My grandfather hadn't taught me how to detect Protestants. "I haven't thought about it. I named one Kovacs and the other Stahl—after Ernie Kovacs and my grandfather—but it doesn't really matter 'cause their last names never come up."

"Kovacs is Hungarian," said Bernie, "and Stahl is German, I think."

"Lousy numbers on both," said Harvey. "You know what our *Hungarian* audience is? And Germans . . . well, all I can say is a lot of guys still remember World War Two."

"But not the audience for this show," I said. "They're all fifteen—and they'll probably flunk their SATs."

"You missed two chances to use Irish and Italian," said the newest man.

"Even if the Hungarian numbers were out there, and they're probably not even out there in *Hungary*, your girls have no nice ghetto flavor," said Sally. "They're so . . . *American*."

"Are Americans 'out' right now?" I said.

"Just Presbyterian types," said the old new man. "There's never been a real hit about a Presbyterian, except maybe *Gone With the Wind*."

"I think she was Catholic," I said.

"Whatever."

"Look, let's face it," said Bud. "Hungarians, Germans, and Presbyterians are all loser minorities. We've gotta go with Italians today."

"I agree," said Bernie. "Ralph, why don't you run the script through one more time and just make that one little change. Make the girls Italians—lower middle class, if you can."

"*Maron*," I softly said.

There are legends about people doomed to do one activity forever: Sisyphus endlessly pushing a rock back up a hill, the Flying Dutchman always at sea, the Wandering Jew never buying a house. And now, as I started to rewrite again, I had the feeling of being all three: wandering Jew forever at sea with a rock of a script I never would finish. I would be no closer to the end merely because the girls were now Rose and Maria. What I had taken on was the labor of a lifetime, a video version of translating the Dead Sea Scrolls. In fact, the Dead Sea Scrolls might have made a better story than the one I was trapped in. Perhaps a lower-middle-class Roman Empire cutie falling in love with a Bedouin boy who had a nice tan. There were no numbers on Bedouins, of course, but Americans did love sheep.

When I had finished changing the blood in my heroines, I sent the script back to Bernie, who called the following week and said, "Your rewrite is great. We'll be taking a meeting on it Monday."

"Terrific," I said. "What time do you want me there?"

"Ralph, I think we'd like to take this one by ourselves. We do that from time to time. We'll keep you posted."

We'll keep you posted. Did that mean he would mail me the name of the writer who was replacing me?

Despondently, I called Artie and said, "How the hell can they have a script meeting without the writer?"

"They think script meetings are better without the writer," he replied. "I guess they feel threatened by you because you keep making sense."

"No, that's not it. They've brought in three more people from the Coast and there's no place for me to sit."

"It's good you can still laugh about all this."

"Which is more than the audience will be doing. You think there'll ever *be* one?"

"Ralph, you've gotten good money for this thing. Now forget it and go back to real writing."

"But is there *any* chance we'll still get a pilot?"

"Well, they have made *one* here in the East, so there's always a chance they'll make another. Meanwhile, start that book about your father. No one'll have to come from the Coast to help you."

I laughed with relief. "I'm starting it in the next five minutes. As soon as I can figure out what the arena should be. You know, my father did like St. Nick's."

The pleasure of starting a book about my father that became *Citizen Paul*, as well as the pleasure of banking a celestial check from CBS, lessened the anxiousness of waiting to be posted by Bernie.

One afternoon, while I used a break in my writing to gaze at the phone, Judy said, "I hate to see you waiting for a call from people who *belong* in a sitcom. Honey, just forget it and think only about your real work."

"The problem is I keep remembering it," I said. "Maybe because it's as much money as I made all last year."

"If you're feeling that kind of pressure, I can go back to teaching. You're home for the girls in the afternoon. Anyway, you're so *wrong* for television: you're the world's worst collaborator."

She had made me sound like Quisling. She had also reminded me that in the beginning, there was the word, not the arena.

A few days later, Bernie finally called and said, "Ralph, I'm afraid we're taking a pass."

There is no phrase I ever have loathed, not even *Fall out with full field packs in fifteen minutes*, not even *Let me see your license and registration*, not even *Have a good day* spoken at night, that I loathe as much as *We're taking a pass*. How I yearn for the pleasant purity of hearing a TV executive say, *We're rejecting your script because we hate it and we hate you and we're not crazy about your mother either.*

"We're just not sure about families right now," he said. But I was sure about mine, about the rating I gave my wife and daughters without wondering what Fred Silverman thought of his, and about the gold I felt I was starting to mine in a book that began:

> "And Johnny, what does *your* father do?"
> "He plays piano in a whorehouse, Teacher."
> "Johnny, how can you *say* such a terrible thing!"
> "Teacher, how can I say he works for Hearst?"
> —Ancient journalism joke

My father never played piano in a whorehouse, but there were many times when I wanted him to audition . . .

ENTR'ACTE

In the summer of 1969, the producer of *Mame* asked me to rewrite the script of a musical about movie stars of the thirties called *Good Good Friends.* Although I felt that a play was a lesser thing than a book, and a musical a lesser thing than a play, and a musical about two thirties stars a lesser thing than *Mr. Ed,* I needed the money and I rationalized that the work might be an interesting challenge.

I was right: it *was* a challenge to rewrite *Good Good Friends* so that no one would know it had been stolen from *Boy Meets Girl.* Unfortunately, the theft had been bungled, for the authors, to use an inappropriate word, had managed to overlook all the humor of *Boy Meets Girl* and instead had contrived a story of a tedious feud between two bitchy middle-aged movie queens. Noel Coward might have been able to keep this fluff airborne with his style, just as Sandy Wilson had done in *The Boy Friend*; but the style of the script I inherited was such that one of its characters was a parody of Carmen Miranda named Siboney del Samba.

Siboney del Samba was as funny as the Miranda law. You cannot parody Carmen Miranda because she parodies *herself*: you cannot launch anything higher than a Brazilian bombshell, except perhaps the Brazilian bomber that started World War II. Moreover, as if this prep school wit was not dreary enough, the show's dialogue was full of lines about chaise longues, draperies, and gowns; I kept expecting a song entitled "Someday My Chintz Will Come."

And so, I began to try to raise a Broadway *Titanic*, ignoring another rule of comic writing: whether gently domestic or wildly farcical, humor must be *about* something—something more than another show; and no amount of surface glitter can hide a hollow or rotten core. You can gift wrap garbage, but the aroma still fills the air.

Writing in the wrong direction—from the outside in, not the inside out—I tried to enrich the book of *Good Good Friends*, pretending that I cared about its two queens; but I soon knew I was in a dead end. At last, I became so desperate that I even reviewed my own theatrical oeuvre in search of something to steal, a fitting thing to do for this show. I had written two plays rather early in my career: one in the sixth grade and one in the seventh, about the shooting of Lincoln and the building of the Panama Canal. Perhaps I could give yellow fever to one of the queens. Better, of course, would have been to give yellow fever to the men who had written this show.

Deciding that neither the death of Lincoln nor the digging of the Panama Canal would have led to a seamless expansion of *Good Good Friends*, I then cut most of the lines about furniture, clothes, and skin care and replaced them with more substantial things that stars might have said to each other in 1933, such as, "Darling, can you *believe* that Von Hindenburg!"

Nevertheless, I was faking it because I didn't know who these women were and a writer should write what he knows. He can, of course, know his imagination: Stephen Crane never saw the Civil War and Richard Rodgers never saw Bali H'ai; but the people, story, and organza of *Good Good Friends* were Novocain for my fancy.

Even though I needed the money I made for ignoring the DO NOT RESUSCITATE sign on *Good Good Friends*, the work was so fruitless and hateful that more than once I cursed Samuel Johnson for saying, *No man but a blockhead ever wrote except for money*. There are limits to nonblockhead writing, Sam: you didn't live to see TV and musical theater. Your dictionary has only one definition for "arena" and only one for "turkey."

7

~

And Tomorrow, Charo and Rudy Hess

I n the fall of 1966, there took place in American letters the most momentous event since Emily Dickinson went out for bread: Jacqueline Susann began to sell a book called *Valley of the Dolls* in a manner previously used for the selling of wind-up dolls. The watershed event, in which so many writers would drown, was not the *publication* of *Valley of the Dolls* but rather its *merchandising* campaign run by Jackie's husband, Irving Mansfield, who told me one day, "You see, there's a *reason* why Jackie is the best writer in America. We go into every big bookstore, buy a few copies of her book, and she inscribes them to the manager and the clerks. Then they put the book in the window and really push it."

Like a dimwitted Greek hearing Archimedes discuss the water in his bathtub, I thought, *Why hadn't I been doing that? Why had I been trying to sell my books to strangers instead of buying them myself and giving them to bookstore clerks as encouragement to sell more to me?*

The answer, of course, was that I would have needed a book improvement loan. The campaign that I *had* been able to wage in the stores had been more modest than Jackie's: each time I published a book, my mother went into Doubleday's, bought one copy, and then called me to say with excitement, "I had to pay full retail. Doesn't Barnes and Noble ever get your books?"

Because Jackie and I happened to share Artie Hershkowitz as our agent, in the years that followed the awesome launching of *Valley of the Dolls*, I was able to see from the inside the full force of her revolution: the bringing of Barnum and Bailey to books.

"We picked this cover for *The Love Machine*," Irving told me one afternoon, "because the colors show up best on TV."

Jackie's books seemed to go not just through editors but Elizabeth Arden's too, and I saw that my mistake had been in giving more thought to my books than to their campaigns. All my covers, for example, seemed to have been designed for public radio.

"I'd love to go down to Atlanta with this one," said Jackie to Artie when *Valley of the Dolls* became the top best-seller, "and pretend to have a car knock me down on the spot where Margaret Mitchell was run over—jokingly, of course."

Artie responded that such publicity might be considered poor taste by cranky purists. To me, however, it seemed that such publicity was only a matter of time, for in America now, it was mattering less what you wrote than how you sold it. The business begun by Hawthorne and Poe was now in the hands of the people with whom I had lunch one day in the spring of 1972.

"We're not publishing this year," said Irving, "because of the presidential election."

For a moment, I wondered if there was something in the Constitution about Jackie, but then Irving explained: "It just takes the play away from us to have all those full-page political ads. Our own full-pagers get lost."

Once again, I was angry at myself, for once again I saw I'd been doing it wrong: *I* foolishly was publishing a book this year, a satire of the sexual revolution called *I Hear America Mating*. And not only had I published during the last two presidential elections, but I had even thrown a book up against the Princeton School Board race. Of course, a union election was enough to distract attention from my books because my publishers had been bringing them out with the style of newsboys on bicycles.

"Aren't you going to take any ads?" I would poignantly say each time.

"No," the publisher would reply, "advertising your book would be a mistake. We think a more intelligent use of the budget would be to concentrate on radio and TV. Doreen has already lined up some terrific call-in shows."

Every writer on a book promotion tour is the illegitimate child of Jackie Susann. I took two such tours BVD (Before *Valley of the Dolls*) and eleven tours in the modern era, but somehow I always managed to be talking just to myself. Irwin Shaw felt that life is ruled by accident, and of course he was right; but my book tours were so rich in accident that it became a basic design and the only accident was when something went right.

My first book tour, the one for *The Block*, took me to Chicago, where I pronounced my name and discussed my book on radio and TV for three days. The fact that Random House had not yet shipped any copies of *The Block* to Chicago gave these interviews a purity that transcended the demeaning vulgarity of a writer hawking his own book; and after I had left the city, it would be two weeks before one copy of my book arrived to sully the belles lettres tone I had set. This aloof little tour, however, was not as pointless as it seemed, for it was excellent training for all the pointless tours to come.

Unfortunately, nothing in Chicago could have prepared me for the opening event of my second book tour, the one for *Time Lurches On*, that began at *The Merv Griffin Show* in New York. While I was sitting in the green room just before the show, trying to memorize lines from my book to ad-lib to Merv, a young woman came in and said, "*Hi*, Mr. Schoenstein, I *loved* your novel!"

"Thanks," I replied, pleased that a reader had found something extra, like a plot, in my book.

"You'll be going on second and we're expecting a terrific show with you and Mr. Fuchida."

"Wonderful," I said. "Who is he?"

"Oh, he led the attack on Pearl Harbor," she said with a merry smile. "It happened in World War Two."

"Yes, near the beginning, I believe. And he's . . . going to be on—with *me?*"

"Well, actually you'll be on with *him* because he's coming out first. His first name is Mitsuo, but the Japanese are more formal than us, so call him Mr. Fuchida and he'll call you Mr. Schoenstein if he can say it. I just *know* the two of you are going to like each other!"

Now in new depths of disbelief, I could hear Merv Griffin saying, *Let's give a really warm welcome to the man who sank the* Arizona—*and so much else . . .*

"Of course, he probably hasn't heard of you," she said, jolting me back to her, "so you may have to lead him."

"The way he led those bombers," I said.

"Yes, but he'd rather not talk too much about World War Two, though I'll tell you one cute thing: he wore red underwear in the attack, so if he did any bleeding, his blood wouldn't show. But now he's a priest of some kind and we'd really rather you didn't talk about the attack or underwear or things like that—*if* Merv keeps him at the desk for you, that is. His message is Christianity now. Is there any of that in your book?"

"I'm afraid I forgot to put it in. But you know, I think Fuchida was the man who cried 'Tora! Tora! Tora!' and that might be a good segue to a story about my bar mitzvah in the book."

"Well, whatever you do, have fun. And better call him *Reverend* Fuchida."

A few minutes later, the show began and Fuchida was revealed at Merv's desk when the curtain went up, thus sparing the audience the need to applaud his entrance, just in case some of the people had been rooting against the Japanese. A pleasant, soft-spoken man, Fuchida did mention the war—it was bound to come up—and he said he was sorry. A magnanimous winner, Merv brushed it all aside, graciously implying, *Heck, anyone can make a mistake.*

I had been looking forward to talking to Fuchida and asking him why his planes had not returned right away and given the rest of Pearl Harbor a lethal second strike; but at the first commercial, he left. He had spent ten minutes selling repentance and now it was time for selling my book.

After my introduction, I walked out on stage to a perfunctory applause by people disappointed to see me instead of someone entertaining. Their evening was skidding downhill, for a contrite war criminal and an unknown writer were hardly a Roman candle opening. And then I sat down with Merv, who pretended to know who I was.

"A remarkable man, that Fuchida," he said, deciding to continue the previous spot rather than grope his way through mine.

"Yes," I said, "but frankly, I can't stop thinking about the *Arizona.*"

"The sunken battleship, yes. Have you ever seen it?"

"No, I haven't. But I once went on the *New Jersey.*"

So far, this interview would have been fine had I been the author of *Jane's Fighting Ships.*

"Tell me, Ralph," he said, "do you think the *Arizona* should be raised?"

"Well, Merv, I don't know, but I tell you this: raising a battleship couldn't be harder than raising children, something I've written about comically in my new book, *Time Lurches On.*"

It was only the start of my second tour, but already I had become a master of the grandly flexible transition, of the happily functional non sequitur.

By the end of this tour, I had seen the competition that a writer faced from his peers on the talk shows and I missed the gentle pacifism of the man who had started World War II. By the end of the tour, I had learned that every week in America more than two hundred books were published, some of them by writers. I suspected that my postman had an outline making the rounds faster than my mail for a compelling blend of religion and sex called *Joan of Arc: Divinity or Dyke?* and my allergist was pitching a memoir called *Nothing to Sneeze At.*

Of making many books there is no end, says the Bible; but even if archaeologists unearth a B. Dalton in Babylon, America today makes B.C. publishing seem like a pushcart press. There is respect among laymen for the talents of musicians, painters, and glassblowers, but *writing* is something that almost everyone knows he can do if he can just find a free weekend, for almost everyone can spell and write a dedication. Moreover, not only are there ninety-seven million writers in America today, but most of them seem to be writing more commercially than I, a fact that has endlessly bothered my mother.

"Can't you ever write something that people actually want to *read?*" she once asked me endearingly. "I mean, that hot new book, *All Creatures Great and Small*—it's just *animal* stories, for God's sake. You and the girls have had *lots* of pets."

"Mom, hamsters and parakeets won't do it," I said.

"Well, there must be some new animal you could find that's cute."

"Mom, the guy who wrote *All Things* is a *veterinarian.*"

"And you're telling me you're not a veterinarian. *I* know that. Neither is Jackie Susann and *she* did a dog book. Maybe she could give you some tips."

"Okay, enough; I'll do it. Let's see . . . I guess I could do a book about . . . hey, the cuteness of indigestion in giraffes. I could call it *All Things Gaseous and Tall.*"

"Just keep it up and Judy will have to take a second job. You just don't see what people want, do you? I mean, you write a sex book with no *sex* in it."

"Mom, that was a *satire* of the sexual revolution."

"People don't want the satire, they want the sex. You've got to stop *laughing* at things like that."

Write longer, said my sister.
Write for regular money, said my father.
Write seriously, said my mother. *Stop laughing.*
And start pretending the world isn't mad.

On *The Mike Douglas Show* with *Time Lurches On,* I stopped laughing for several minutes, defeated by a mouth even better at sabotaging conversation than mine. I had flown to this show, then done in Cleveland, to share a half hour with Cleveland Amory, who was promoting a book on animals that my mother had told me to write. Each of us was to have about twelve minutes to sell his book to all the people who were watching afternoon television instead of painting by the numbers.

When the show began, Amory and I were sitting with Mike Douglas in a gazebo, where my segment was to come first. Turning to me, Mike said, "Ralph, there's a chapter in your new book about the censoring of nursery rhymes. Tell us what's happened to the Big Bad Wolf."

"*I'll* tell you what's happened to the wolf," said Amory, "and many other animals too. I'm here to say it's an outrage."

He was also there to say it second, but no longer: the fate of the wolf was no more outrageous than the way that Amory, a fierce foe of vivisection, now carved up my time. While I sat there helplessly wondering what I might say if I could ever enter the talk about what I'd thought was my book, Amory held up an animal trap that I wished he were in. And for the next twenty minutes, all of which I devoted to silent dismay, millions of people thought about muskrats and otters instead of my children.

In Chicago three years later, while touring with another book, I was conversationally mugged again.

"Well, Kup," I said to a television host named Irv Kupcinet, "I decided to write about London bridge because—"

"Oh, *I* had a bridge made in London!" said Hermione Gingold. "But all my inlays were done right here." And then she held the stage for ten minutes, while I envisioned a dentist attending to her with a pneumatic drill.

However, I kept learning; and by the time that my seventh book came out, I had raised non sequitur to an art form and could detour any conversation into a cold-blooded sales pitch. In fact, if my telephone had rung and a strange man had whispered, "How much for a night under the covers with your sister?" I instantly would have replied, "My sister is already under the covers of my new book, *Wasted on the Young*, which I'm sure your prison library will have."

A challenge just as formidable as the foul transitions of enemy writers was the style of the talk show hosts who pretended to interview me. When *Yes, My Darling Daughters* came out, my publisher sent me to Minneapolis, saying it was "a good book town"; but he must have meant a love for the Bible, for I sensed no literary ambience as I sat in the green room of *Twin Cities Today* and watched the guest who preceded me perform his act: making music by blowing air into a plumber's tool.

This, I thought, is the place of the writer in America: following the Heifetz of the toilet in America's good book town.

The audience, however, was so delighted by this earthy musician that he was asked to do a few encores, thus reducing the length of my segment. As a writer, I was accustomed to having my time eroded by actors, criminals, and whores, but I had never followed an act that literally was down the drain, the spot so often reserved for me.

As I sat there listening to the encores, an assistant producer ran in and said, "Can you give me a couple of questions that Dewey can ask you? Just in case. Of course, he *might* be able to go the full six minutes with what he has because he's really into books this week."

"I've already given three questions to someone else," I told her. "I hope I remember the answers."

"You're on, Mr. Schoenman!" said the stage manager moments later, and I walked out to face a few hundred people who hated me for lowering the quality of their entertainment by talking about a book.

"So you're the author of *All My Darling Daughters*," said the host, almost reading a cue card.

"Yes, Dewey, I am," I replied.

"A terrific read; I'm almost through it."

"Thanks."

"You're an expert on child-raising, sort of like Lee Salk?"

"Well, he has a Ph.D., but I'm still living with my children."

"Your book . . . we could say it's sort of like *Eight Is Enough*."

"It's six children fewer than *Eight Is Enough*, but that may be fixed for the paperback. My wife just had another daughter."

"Cute, that's really cute."

"Yes, she—"

"You know, *I* have a book I'm going to knock off one of these days."

"And I've always wanted to knock off a talk show."

"Cute again; I *like* talking about books. You got any more of 'em coming down the pike?"

"Nothing I can talk about right now, but something is always gestating."

"Hey, that's your *wife's* department. But a labor of *love*, right? Ralph, I'm afraid we're almost out of time. But before you go, do you have any child-raising advice for the Twin Cities?"

"Well, I think children here are a lot like the ones in other places. And it seems to me there are really no absolute rules for raising them."

"I agree, but give us three."

"Okay, love 'em . . . and listen to 'em . . . and be patient. And with all that, you still need luck: it's always a roll of the dice."

"And that's snake eyes for the author's corner today. Many thanks, Ralph Schoenstein, for sharing all your wisdom with us. Tomorrow in the author's corner, another big one: we'll be meeting Ronnie DuBoff, whose blockbuster exposé of Mother Teresa, *Semi-Pious,* has particular meaning for the Twin Cities."

My promotional style in the bookstores continued to be just as effective as my promotional style on TV. By 1980, the small bookstores of my early days, where the clerks had never heard of my books, were being replaced by giant chains, where the clerks had never heard of books. No clerk at Walden's had ever heard of *Walden;* and the looks on their faces had a bright new blankness whenever I dropped my incognito guise and revealed myself as a writer of a new book.

"I'd like a copy of *Citizen Paul,*" I said one day to a young woman at the front desk of a Dalton's after digging a path through the Ludlums, Micheners, and Kings.

Looking up from her copy of *Teen Beat,* she replied, "*Citizen Paul?* Is that something about the Pope?"

"No, it's my ninth crucifixion."

"Your what?"

"Sorry, just kidding—like my career."

Judy had said more than once that what was left of my mind would someday snap in a bookstore, and it seemed that the moment had arrived.

"There was a rave review for it in *Publishers Weekly,*" I told her.

"Oh yeah, I've heard of that," she said. "What's the name of the book again?"

"*Citizen Paul.* It's about a father and a son."

"Maybe look in child care. Does it have an author?"

"Yes, it does: Ralph Schoenstein."

"Never heard of him. I'll check our computer to see if it's been published."

"Believe me, it *has.* Look, if you do happen to have it, I'd like to buy a copy for you."

"For *me?* Hey, that's nice. If we don't have it, how about the new Jackie Collins instead?

What a fool I've been all these years, I thought. *Trying to sell my books in the worst possible place: a bookstore.* Smiling sadly at the young custodian of the nation's new literature, I turned and walked away, aware that this particular absurdity was merely tied to my life's work. Children were still being run over by drunks and an earthquake had just killed thousands in Iran, so it was hardly a significant tragedy that America's bookstores were now being run by the maids of the mall. As I had said to Dewey while he checked his hair, my family was still together and seemingly good ideas for new books to be buried still were coming to me, in showers and ballparks and buses and even operating rooms.

A few months before my descent into Dalton's, I had gone to a hospital for a hernia repair. Because I was now a better writer than I had been at the time of my tendon repair, I was able to smuggle into surgery better supplies: a tiny pencil from miniature golf less obvious than my tendon Scripto had been, and also a small notebook. Was it idiotic to be planning to make notes at my own operation? Only if I were going to be given a general anesthetic; but this surgeon was giving me a local and I didn't want to spoil his work by squirming the way I had done in jail when having no pencil to record my ideas.

As the orderlies moved me from the gurney to the operating table, I managed to hold the pencil and notebook against my thigh; and then, to my delight, the surgeon revealed that he was attuned to the literary life.

"Ralph, I'll bet you can get a good story out of this," he said, echoing all the people who felt that writers did everything just to create material. It happened, however, that on this particular occasion, I had not ruptured myself so that my groin could be grist for the mill. In spite of my pencil and pad, this was one of those odd moments when I was actually living life for its own sake, as I had done when proposing to Judy and getting dysentery in East Pakistan.

"I was right: I see you've started writing the story," said the surgeon, glancing at my pencil and notebook while the anesthetist began the drip of my IV. "You know, *I* have a book that I've always been meaning to bat out. A lot of funny things happen in here."

"They do?" I said, suddenly wondering why I hadn't simply settled for a truss.

"Yes, and I've already got the title. What do you think about *It's Not My Table?*"

"Cute." Was I already past the point of no return on the IV?

"Or do you prefer *Your Table Is Ready?* The first one is more commercial, of course, but it might be saying I have no responsibility for my patients."

"And you *do*, right?"

"Of course; it would just be literary license. And I don't have to tell *you* about that."

It was his medical license I was wondering about as he began to slice my groin.

"You know, Ralph," he said, "A. J. Cronin, Somerset Maugham, and Arthur Conan Doyle all were doctors."

"Yes, I know. Are you a doctor too?"

"Hey, that's good. I can use it in the book."

In early 1982, to supplement my income from magazine pieces, Op Ed pieces, and nonreturnable book advances, I joined a lecture bureau, the Program Corporation of America, that had asked me to entertain at colleges with a talk based on *Alma Matters*, my new paperback on how to survive college life. My fee would be fifteen hundred dollars, one third of which would go to the bureau and all of which was about fifteen thousand dollars less than the fees being given to certain Republican parolees, who were now amusing students with tales of how they had tried to destroy the government of the United States. Hermann Goering and Hirohito might have gotten twenty.

The fact that G. Gordon Liddy was being paid twice as much as Benjamin Spock said something fundamental about America in the eighties; and something fundamental also would be coming from me: as the Preface to *Alma Matters* said:

> Whether you are now embarked upon realizing or avoiding your potential, four wonderful years lie ahead. But college lies ahead too, for everyone goes to college today, even people who want to learn things.

Lecturing seemed to make sense for me now, even though little else had. By lecturing, perhaps I could finally paddle out of my private creek and enter the literary mainstream, for John Updike had said, "People are becoming more and more illiterate and we are returning to an oral culture." And so, perhaps it was time for me to start sparing people the strain of having to process the words I foolishly had put on paper instead of on cue cards or audiotape.

One morning in the spring of 1983, as I incredulously approached my fiftieth birthday, an agent at the Program Corporation of America gave me my first chance to enter the literary mainstream.

"Southeastern Oklahoma State University wants you to speak," she said.

My momentary pause must have revealed a certain disappointment. Southeastern Oklahoma State—did they call it Old SOS?—not only wasn't Ivy League, it was probably full of crop dusting majors, a safety school for kids who couldn't get into Northeast Iowa Tech. Nevertheless, I needed the money, for Eve-Lynn was now in college herself and I was still repaying loans for sending Jill. A man named Donald Regan, one of the Lilliputian minds around Ronald Reagan, had recently said, "Whatever happened to the old-fashioned idea of working your way through college?" He was unaware that the only part-time jobs that my daughters could have used to give them twenty thousand dollars a year would have been field representatives for the Medellín cartel.

"Where is Southeastern Oklahoma State University?" I asked the agent, fearing it was in southeastern Oklahoma.

"It's in Durant, down the road from Dallas," she said. "And I want you to know that they're really happy to be getting you."

Had Mitsuo Fuchida and Minnie Pearl turned them down?

Six weeks later, at the Dallas airport, I was met by Lyman Beggs, a very tall member of the Southeastern Oklahoma State University Student Council, who graciously led me to my ground transportation: a Chevrolet pickup truck. Because the back of the truck was empty, I wondered if we would be stopping for alfalfa on our way. We would have sufficient time to find some, for it was ninety-seven miles down the road from Dallas to Durant.

As we drove out of Dallas, I drew Lyman into talk about the school and learned that he, like most of the students, was a Baptist; and he was deeply curious about alien creeds because he suddenly asked me one of the two most memorably unanswerable questions of my life. The first had come in 1970 from Joe Franklin, who had said on the air, "Ralph is a *columnist*. Ralph, do a column." I was still trying to find an answer to Joe when Lyman Beggs said, "Mr. Schoenstein, you're Jewish, aren't you?"

This was not the unanswerable question: this was an easy true-false one and I correctly said, "Right."

"Well, I gotta tell you, I never met a Jewish person and I've always kinda wondered: How does it *feel* to be Jewish?"

I found myself unable to be offended by the question because there was something sweetly moronic about Lyman that touched me while I was being depressed. Moreover, although I was tempted to tell him that being Jewish felt almost the same as if I had been a human being, I feared that levity might confuse a mind that had all it could handle in shifting from second into third.

"It feels fine, especially now that the Pope has acquitted me of killing Jesus," I said, helping his study of the pagan world while asking myself: *If the college chose* him *to escort its speaker, what were the* other *students like? Would* their *questions come before or after show-and-tell?*

About an hour later, after our talk had turned from Hebraic consciousness to the deeper question of whether man was meant to have steroids shrink his testicles, we entered Oklahoma, my first visit to the state. At once, I began looking for corn to see if it was as high as an elephant's eye, but I couldn't find any, perhaps because this was May.

"Is the corn here really as high as an elephant's eye?" I said to Lyman.

"We got no elephants," he replied.

"I mean as they say in *Oklahoma!*"

"I never heard no one in Oklahoma say that."

"I mean *Oklahoma!* the *show,* the musical classic."

· "'Fraid I don't know that one."

"Gee, it should be so famous here. In fact, it's your official state *song* and you've never *heard* of it?"

"No, sir. But I sure liked *Grease Two.*"

When Lyman and I reached the SOS campus in the late afternoon, he took me to a motel to rest until my eight o'clock talk at Montgomery Auditorium, where, in memory of my grandfather, I would open this territory to his people. In my room, after taking a shower, I found a Bible and thought about my daughter Lori, now seven, who called this book a "holly Bible," as if it were Scripture wrapped in a wreath. While I lay on the bed, I turned to Ecclesiastes and read about the transience of things, not the merriest diversion, for it enriched the melancholy I already felt at being a religious relic in a backwater of Baptists. I would have been wiser to read something more cheerful, like the fire code on the door.

At ten after seven, I left the motel for a leisurely walk that would lead me in a roundabout way to Montgomery Auditorium, for I had always loved to stroll across college campuses and wistfully lose myself in their leafy hopefulness. I was walking now beneath the early evening stars, which became a song cue: I was thinking about their getting blurry above the surrey with the fringe on top.

Here was one of my problems: I had always believed all the songs. I did not, of course, believe that the gates of heaven were guarded by United States Marines or even by burly altar boys; but I did believe that the things we did last summer, we'll remember all winter long; and I believed that a fella needs a girl to sit by his side at the end of a weary day; and I believed that though there's one motor gone, we can still carry on.

But could *I* still carry on, a rocky romantic who too often had tried to live life thirty-two bars at a time? Now, nearing fifty, I felt no more adult than the boy who had conducted Beethoven in his bedroom; but I had no old-fashioned melodies for AIDS or the hole in the ozone or any of the other entries on the doomsday hit parade.

Strolling across the campus, past teenagers who thought Pearl Harbor had the new number-one single, I thought of my own college days and was suddenly even more dismayed by the passage of time than by the thought of an absurd and indifferent universe full of accidents and lawyers. The passage of time left me gasping, for each day I moved further away from the sweet frozen frames of my family photos. I realized again that much of my writing had been an attempt to preserve the past and make sense of it while wondering if it had been but a dream. Why couldn't time's winged chariot have been a trolley car instead? Why couldn't the Greek philosopher who said "All is flux" have said "All is flax" or "All should floss" or *anything* other than the thought that nothing but worrying ever lasts? For if nothing lasted, then did anything matter, even the Mets' hunt for a third baseman or Lori at the piano gliding through the glory of Bach? Suddenly, I wanted to be walking not beside John the Baptist, but to be pushing Jill in her stroller to play with bunnies at her nursery school in the year that I was thirty-one.

Was Oklahoma a good place for me to crack up? Yes, the ideal place: just down the road from the Menninger Clinic. Perhaps the clinic would have bunnies for *me*.

As if these thoughts of time and terror were not dismaying enough, I was also bedeviled by the writer's favorite worry: What next? Every time I finished something, especially a book, I would quietly muse, *Christ, that's it: I'll never think of anything else and I'm too old to reenlist.* In spite of all the good ideas that already had come to me, I kept feeling this panic. My oeuvre continued to grow, but every egg I laid felt like the final one, even though a humorist is luckier than most other writers: what he says is less important than how he says it, so he can feel free to treat a subject that has been done more than once before, as I did when I looked at tourism in *With T-Shirts & Beer Mugs for All,* at sex in *I Hear America Mating,* at family life in *Yes, My Darling Daughters,* and at the worship of youth in *Wasted on the Young.*

And now, fighting my private demons at a little college in Oklahoma, it was time to see if I could keep the young from wasting me.

By eight o'clock, the time that my talk was supposed to begin, I had managed to regain my grip, deciding that some things simply *had* to matter, even if this talk wasn't one. I was standing now at a corner of the Montgomery Auditorium stage, trying to look lost in intellect while I counted the house, a task that needed just a few seconds. Almost forty people, more than twenty of whom were students, had grabbed the center orchestra seats in a theater that held twelve hundred. Often in my writing I had felt I was talking to myself; and now, befitting the change from a written to an oral culture, I'd be talking to myself fashionably.

"I'm really sorry we don't have more people for you tonight," said Lyman, approaching from backstage. "A lot of 'em have exams."

"Oh, that's okay; studying comes first," I said. For a writer, even more important than knowing English is knowing how to take humiliation. "Maybe I could just take everyone out for coffee."

"You wanna wait till a few more come?"

"Well, I have to be home by Friday . . ."

"Right."

"And if we wait for more, some of *these* might go."

"Right. Look, you gotta come back again, hear? Last month, we really filled the place for Maureen Dean."

Moments later, Lyman stood before the assembled handful and presented me.

"It's a real honor to have with us here tonight Mr. Ralph Schoenstein, a writer and an author who . . ."

People sometimes wonder about the difference between a writer and an author. The answer, of course, is that an author is a dead writer; and on this night in Oklahoma, I was definitely an author, one looking down at a partial microcosm of an audience, whose male members no doubt were nostalgic for the literary uplift of Maureen Dean's breasts.

As I came to the podium, I was almost in focus for students who had been part of a national survey revealing that twenty-four percent of them didn't know when Columbus had landed—and then, of course, had gone on to discover San Diego; and forty-two percent of them thought that the American Civil War was one of the traumas of the twentieth century.

Nevertheless, I started my talk, wondering why. After saying some things about my work, as familiar to these students as the Rosetta Stone, I decided to try to wake them up by reading a bit of *Alma Matters* called Your English Placement Test:

1) Giving a job to a relative is called

    (a) nepotism.
    (b) nationalism.
    (c) incest.

2) Conjunctivitis is

    (a) the uncontrollable urge to conjugate.
    (b) the excessive use of conjunctions.
    (c) no worse than VD.

3) Which of the following is correct?

(a) My sister is an easy lay and that's no lie.
(b) My sister likes to lie on her lei.
(c) My sister likes to lie in the loo.

4) Syntax is

(a) a Japanese camera.
(b) a tampon.
(c) speaking good.

While I was delivering this nonsense, only some of the adults in the audience were laughing; the students responded as if I were reading from Deuteronomy. I long had known, of course, about the great subjectivity in savoring humor, for I had been writing in America, a nation that will one day be known as the nation that laughed at Pee Wee Herman; but in spite of this demoralizing range of taste in humor, I had the uneasy feeling that some of these students weren't laughing because they were taking me seriously. Once again, I was drilling for Feldman Oil, a fitting venture in Oklahoma.

For many years, *Playboy* had written "Humor" over the titles of my pieces, although this label had never been put on Hugh Hefner's philosophy; and now I needed that label again, flashing in neon, or else I needed students who knew that nepotism wasn't a matter for the police. Were some of these young people preparing to run bookstores? I sensed that the wit they wanted was John Belushi playing with food, not some scrawny stranger playing with words.

The moment I had finished my bombing run, I spared the students the decision of whether or not to applaud by quickly saying, "Okay, now how about some questions?"

I was asking for trouble. I was asking for someone to say, "Why did the school get you instead of a *real* speaker?" At least no one would want me to tell her where the scatter rugs were.

"Yes," I said with a smile, pointing to a young man in the front row of the audience, which wasn't far from the back row.

"Is *Alma Matters* your first book?" he said, having forgotten both Lyman's introduction and my entire talk.

"No, it's my fourteenth."

"Did you ever write anything I heard of?"

"Well, what have you heard of?"

"I mean best-sellers."

"Oh, I don't sell to just *anybody*. I always try to be selective."

A few adults laughed, but the young man didn't: he looked perplexed and I regretted being facetious to him. I had always liked talking to students and still hoped that there were some in the hall.

"Yes," I said, pointing to a young woman.

"Do you ever write anything serious?"

I thought of E. B. White's words: *Every humorist can recall the day when some loved one anxiously asked him when he was "going to write something serious."* And I thought of Walter Matthau, who was asked, "When are you going to do something serious?" and replied, "My serious stuff is my comedy." And I thought of my father killing a column of mine that had spoofed advertising, even though one by Jim Bishop had just solemnly made the same point. "But it's less dangerous to say it *his* way," my father had said when I'd brandished the inconsistency. "Why can't *you* ever be serious?"

With a smile intended to indicate wisdom, I looked down at the young woman and said, "A familiar question. I don't want to sound teachy, but I will anyway because this seems like a school. Most of my humor has been basically serious on another level, especially my personal stuff, like my books about my father and my children and my boyhood. And my novel about the worship of youth was pretty serious too. You see, you've got to have *both* these dimensions to make the writing really worthwhile."

Her eyes were starting to glaze, while some of her friends no doubt were wishing that they could have been studying for a calculus exam or having calculus removed from their teeth.

"What misleads a lot of people," I said, letting pass a splendid opportunity to shut up, "is that a humorist has an irreverent point of view and a comical style in what he's saying that . . . and this is *ironic*—I mean, E. B. White says that good humorous writing has *extra* content because it plays close to the fire of truth."

"Evie who?" she said.

"No, *Mister* E. B. White."

"Who's he?"

ENTR'ACTE

Good writing is *rewriting*, something I like doing on an old steel German typewriter with my wooden Hungarian head. I appreciate the wonder of a computer; but not even the Japanese will ever make a word processor better than the mind of a disciplined writer doing draft after draft to find the right words. You do not have to be Flaubert, spending an entire day of syntactical anguish in search of one word; but some mental stretching *is* required if you want your work to sound different from that of the Newark high school principal who wrote, *There will be a modified English course offered for those children who achieve a deficiency in English.*

America has achieved a deficiency in English so grand that I laugh out loud whenever I receive a letter urging that English be made our national language. Of *course* English should be made our national language, and we should drop the one now in use, the one used by the American Savings Bank, which recently said to me:

Dear Policyholder:

There has been some changes in our S.B.L.I. policies. At certain ages the premium of our new policies are lower than those issued in prior years.

*   *   *

I wish Mark Twain were here to read those two sentences, for they contain, pound for pound, as many offenses against English as Twain had found in the work of that distinguished literary criminal, James Fenimore Cooper.

Even more depressing than this savings and loan illiteracy is a line in a letter to me from the Emerson Literary Society of Hamilton College:

> As far as general campus news, a faculty committee recently came out with a report on private societies and ELS showed the greatest increase in grade point average after joining.

A writer today must fiercely resist such contagion; and it would also be nice if he knew my favorite literary tip from Mark Twain: *The difference between the right word and almost the right word is the difference between lightning and a lightning bug.*

Thus Twain has supplied my final advice: Go for the lightning, not the bugs, because only in sparkling execution does humor come alive. No other form of prose so mercilessly demands the precise placement of precisely the right words in felicitous order. Pardon the pompous ring of this point: all writers, of course, seek the right words, even writers who try to make douching seem like a walk in the moonlight; but the right words are more important in humor than in the memoirs of Fats Domino, a point I beat to the ground earlier by deflating a section of "Look for the Rusty Lining."

In *The Importance of Being Earnest*, a servant says, "I have only been married once. That was in consequence of a misunderstanding between myself and a young woman." If Oscar Wilde had written, "That was in consequence of a misunderstanding between a young woman and myself," the line would have been a lightning bug; but Wilde was in touch with the heavens, as was the author of "Wagner's music is not as bad as it sounds." Note that he did not say, "Wagner's music is better than it sounds" or "Wagner's music doesn't stink like you think." And note that George S. Kaufman said, "Try everything in life except incest and folk dancing." Had the incest come last, it would have been a dull coupling indeed.

Humor needs style even more than substance—Nabokov, in fact, said "Style *is* matter"—and style to me is a voice speaking with a uniqueness that seems as inevitable as it is delightful. I have always found strength in Raymond Chandler's saying: *The most durable thing in writing is style.*

The power of the perfect word is sadly clear to me each December, when I have to keep hearing the damaged "Have Yourself a Merry Little Christmas." In *Meet Me in St. Louis*, the song's strongest line had been the bittersweet "Until then we'll have to muddle through somehow." However, in their infinite ignorance, record producers changed the line to "Hang a shining star upon the highest bough," thus giving the climax of the song all the poetic elegance of "Sh-Boom."

My own lightning rod, even when the weather was foggy, has always been a pencil grounded to a pad. Unable to write orally, I have to keep seeing the words evolve on paper, a quirk unknown to a producer named Bud Yorkin when he optioned my satirical novel, *Wasted on the Young*, and brought me to Hollywood to write the screenplay.

On the plane to Los Angeles, I said to myself, *Okay, what's the arena? Do movies use arenas? I'll have to find out.* I had never written a movie, but I felt I could do dialogue. I was, after all, the writer whose Lincoln had turned to his wife and said, "Mary, I think I've been shot. It hurts. It hurts real bad." Mine was a Lincoln who spoke colloquially, even with a bullet in his brain.

I had been in Bud Yorkin's office no more than five minutes, wondering if he liked the white loafers that Judy had bought for me, when he said, "So what do you think about the opening scene?"

Because my only thought about the opening scene was that it should come first, I replied, "Well . . . I really think it has to get things going."

"What should *happen* in it?"

And then I realized that he wanted to start to write the screenplay right there at his desk, talking it out with a nondictator in white shoes.

I looked at him with nervous eyes and a numb imagination. This was no mere writer's block: this was a whole neighborhood, for talking wasn't writing to me. I was the man who disliked most conversations because they were bad first drafts. I was the man who changed a word in the middle of a page of final copy and then retyped the entire page, happy for the chance to do one more draft. No platoon sergeant was ever more in love with polishing than I.

"Bud," I said uneasily, "would it be okay if . . . I went into the conference room and worked out the first scene on a pad?"

He looked at me as if I had just requested a night in bed with his cocker spaniel; in Hollywood, a pad is for a waiter.

"Well . . . all right," he said. "But think cinematically."

"Absolutely. I am a camera."

Once in the conference room, liberated from the pressure of asking the muses to move my mouth instead of my hand, I roughed out an opening scene, rewrote it a couple of times, and took it to Yorkin, who liked everything in it but the dialogue.

"This isn't what these people should be saying," he told the man who had conceived them. "Now here in the lab . . . suppose Randy says . . ."

As he orally revised the scene, I tried again to write with my voice, but I was unbalanced by the tentativeness of it all and I lacked confidence in lines I was dropping into the creative quicksand. I kept waiting to hear Yorkin say, *Let's put Randy in an all-girls high school, one that has arena football.*

That night in my hotel, feeling as de Gaulle had felt about collaborators, I wrote another scene, reading the lines aloud to make sure they were not too literary. I had my characters pausing, stammering, and clearing their throats; and I was even tempted to have one of them choke on his food. The trick, I decided, was to use no complete sentences, so the director and actors would have something to finish, like a dot-to-dot book.

The following morning, I took the scene to Yorkin, a director himself.

"Your problem is," he said, "that you're too concerned with language."

He had turned the passion of my life into an insult that made me feel good.

Five days later, a former screenwriter flying back to my Underwood, I began a new piece of prose, feeling again the deep delight of seeing words that could be fixed on a page; and also the delight of knowing that the stewardess would not be sitting down beside me and saying, "By the way, in your Lincoln play—that shooting business—why not have him say, 'And I thought the *war* was a headache!'"

8

~

Forever Cleveland

As if written for that Oklahoma student who had asked about Evie White, my next two books, *Every Day Is Sunday* and *Diamonds for Lori and Me*, were the most serious ones I had done, though I felt that they were my funniest too; and each of them had the potential to sell dozens of copies, unless I could find a way to avoid using bookstores, for the publishing giantism of the eighties made Jackie Susann seem like Emily Dickinson. A piece in *The Times* said that books were now being written, packaged, and promoted the way that McDonald's sold Big Macs. In such a world, I was salted peanuts.

Every Day Is Sunday was my lighthearted journey through those maximum security playgrounds called leisure villages; and *Diamonds for Lori and Me* was the story of how my youngest daughter and I had found the happiest hiding place: a baseball field. As if in response to my own Oklahoma question about anything that lasted and mattered, baseball had seemed to last with a timeless sweetness that Lori and I had embraced in a world whose baroque lunacy was still unknown to her and too well known to me. Moreover, on a less metaphysical level, I wrote these two books because I was too stupid to give up and find more sensible work, like designing tattoos. As homework for an English teacher who had asked how Thomas A. Edison resembled anyone in the student's family, Lori had written:

> Edison never gave up and neither does my Dad. He writes books and even though most of them weren't best sellers, he always goes right back and writes another one.

Why? is what many wanted to know. Was *Every Day Is Sunday* my incandescent bulb and *Diamonds for Lori and Me* my phonograph? Or were they my glowworm and my kazoo?

"Barnes and Noble still doesn't have them," my mother had said.

Every Day Is Sunday was my tour of America's major leisure villages, a look at the segregation of older people in a country where the seven ages of man were now preschooler, Pepsi generation, baby boomer, mid-lifer, empty-nester, senior citizen, and organ donor. America was now a place where the worship of youth had moved me to write:

> The message kept coming at me: Cover my spots and erase my lines and color my hair and use the Anti-Aging Diet to chew my way to yesterday. The message never stopped: Get *younger*, get *younger!* Tote that cream and lift that face! I had been going in the wrong *direction* by awakening each morning one day older.

Because I knew of no other personal adventure in the leisure villages, I finished the book with the feeling that I had explored new territory; and the manuscript was well received, though not by my publisher. Howard Teichman called it "wonderfully witty

and brilliantly bittersweet," Herbert Tarr called it "a funny, illuminating account of the after life in leisure villages and the
author's own inner life," and Little, Brown called it too short
and deducted five thousand dollars from the second half of my
advance. My own publisher had joined the public in using a
postal scale to determine the worth of a book.

"It's a warm feeling to have my own house behind me," I
told Gene Young, my fine editor at Little, Brown. "But at least
it's just a penalty and not also interest like the IRS."

"Ralph, I love the book; you know that," she replied. "But
everyone here thought you'd be writing a more comprehensive
guide to all these places. That's what your outline said."

"True, it did; but Gene, a book takes a life of its own in the
writing—if it's any good."

"This one took a life outside the contract."

I sighed. "Yes, I know what you're saying. You'd probably
rather have a leisure village *Yellow Pages*."

"The problem is we just can't classify what you've written."

"A *book*! A book in English!"

She laughed. "*You* know what I mean: it doesn't fit into any
category."

"But Gene, isn't that the whole *point* of writing: to be
original?"

"Specifically original, not *generically*. There's just too big a
gap between what was promised and what was delivered. How
are the salesmen going to *sell* this book?"

"But there *is* a lot of reporting under the entertainment: the
reader is having fun *and* learning things. Can't the stores sell
that?"

"Where do they *put* it? Under humor? Under travel? Under
aging?"

"Under the counter. There's a big shelf of my books down
there."

"The fact that it's funny actually weakens it for sales. Ralph,
people want information more than entertainment."

I pictured fifty million Americans dialing 411 in an orgy of

uplift, a nation of grimly merry self-improvers, whose philosopher, Calvin Coolidge, had said, *The business of America is
business.*

"It's too bad that Ralph can't get into a nice little business
and write on the side," Judy's mother had told her once a
month.

But I *was* in a nice little business: limited editions; and I was
doing something *more* than writing on the side: I was writing on
the edge. I was a full-time, free-lance humorist, blithely ignoring the words of E. B. White, the well-known Dallas draft
choice, about decorating our serious writers with laurels and our
wags with Brussels sprouts.

And if you were both? Five thousand less lettuce.

Every Day Is Sunday was the third book in which I had both
explored and reacted to a major part of American life. This
time, however, the exploration shook me and caused a scene in
Sun City, Arizona that showed why Alfred Alvarez had said,
"Writing is the most dangerous of professions."

Early one evening in September of 1985, after spending a day
with the Sun City people, I was sitting with Judy in a lounge of
our motel while Lori played the piano.

"She's playing like a teenager," I said. "God. In only nine
years, she'll be in college and we'll be alone. We'll be able to
start doing things all by ourselves."

"A life of our own?" said Judy with a wry smile. "That's
pretty self-indulgent, I'd say."

"But be honest: nothing has been more fun for us than the
girls—right?"

"I wouldn't know. We've never *tried* anything else."

"Just nine years . . . they're going so fast."

My eyes took on a mistiness that was the look of either a poet
or a basset hound.

"Are you about to start reminiscing again? If so, I'm going to
walk over there and start talking to that man about his bypass.
It'll be fresher than another trip down memory lane with you."

"Okay, okay, I'll stay in the present." I turned toward the man she had mentioned and looked for some sign of life. "Jesus, that's too old to be. Let's really try to avoid that age."

"Only Barbies stay the same age."

"I know; it's just that doing this book has made me even more aware of time. I mean, how did Willie Mays get to be fifty-four?"

"You know, *you're* what's wrong with this country: always trying to stay young. That novel you wrote about finding a youth drug—the hero was *you*. And all that *stuff* you take: Vitamin C and E and brewer's yeast and zinc . . . What's next? Antifreeze?"

She had me squirming now. I wondered if the exercise was good for my circulation.

"And checking the *Enquirer* in the A&P," she said, "to see if some woman of a hundred has had a baby or if someone can remember seeing Lincoln."

"I find hope where I can," I said, trying to lighten things but feeling ashamed.

"What you want to do is stop time. Well, life isn't a basketball game."

"You've been reading Schopenhauer."

"You know what I'll tell the judge? That I've been married to Ponce de Leon. Who only found Fort Lauderdale, as I recall."

"Honey, I just can't help it: I'm a writer and writers spend a lot of time in the past; it's risky business."

"Well, a writer should know that thousands of children are starving to death in Africa. They're having their midlife crises at *three*, so I guess they won't be looking for wrinkles or clipping ads for Hungarian bee pollen. It seems to *me* that anyone who's allowed to get older should have no complaints."

"Yes, of course, of *course*," I said, taking her hand. "I felt stupid clipping that ad. And I *know* you can't trust the Hungarians."

"Well, maybe their bees are okay."

"And maybe I'll be okay too."

We both were silent for a few seconds, and then she squeezed my hand.

"Honey, *I* know how you feel," she said. "I heard 'English Country Garden' the other day and it made me sad 'cause I remembered taking Jill to see Captain Kangaroo."

"That lovely song. She was two."

"And now they've taken him off the air."

"That's what I mean: nothing lasts, not the Morosco Theater or the Astor Hotel or even Captain Kangaroo. It's a disposable world."

"But you can't let it make you crazy. That look in your eyes whenever you hear, *Where is the little girl I carried?*"

"Lori is almost too heavy for me now. My hauling days are ending; I've run out of thirty-pound girls. You know, sometimes I think I'd be happiest in a job where I could just carry little children around."

"Like kidnapping."

"No, I should've been a fireman. It's also less risky than being a writer."

"You really *are* the catcher in the rye."

"Or the shortstop."

"But remember where he ended up."

Three years later, on a steamy evening in mid-August of 1988, I was in an elegant Cleveland hotel with Lori, now twelve, who had come with me on a quasi-promotional tour for my new book about the love for baseball that had made us kids together. *Diamonds for Lori and Me* concerned what had shaken me in Sun City: What could I hold on to in a world of terrifying randomness and truly annoying flux? Lori had helped me to find the answer and also a way to reenter a cherished part of my past: in our noisy sanctuary at Shea Stadium, she had given my boyhood back to me:

On that intoxicating day when Lori fell in love with the Mets, when she added her voice to the thousands who sang "Take Me Out to the Ball Game" as if it were the national anthem, I owed nine thousand dollars to the Internal Revenue Service and my dentist had been discussing canals with the glee of Teddy Roosevelt at Panama. But I knew that I was safe, that nothing bad could happen to a man at a baseball game, especially when beside him a daughter with mustard-stained lips was demanding, "Let's go, Mets!"

The next night at dinner, Lori's ponytail was hidden by her Mets cap, and the figures on her mind were not math homework but the batting averages of her new heroes.

"Gary Carter is really in a clump," she told me.

"That's *slump*, honey," I replied.

"A clump is worse than a slump," she said.

I instantly knew that clump was a splendid new word. Not only was my little girl in love with the world's greatest game, but she also was enriching its language the way Red Barber did when I was a boy. What *son* could have done any better! I felt as elated as if Lori had just won a spelling bee. And she *could* have won a spelling bee, for she knew that there were three o's in Mooo-kie.

Once again, I was feeling the dreamy absurdity of my life. Twenty-three years after coming to Cleveland to fall into an animal trap on *The Mike Douglas Show*, I was back here for another underground sale of a book. I had found *two* constants in an inconstant world: baseball and pointless publicity. Perhaps in another twenty-three years, I'd return to Cleveland like a lost locust and buzz the bookstore again. No, there would *be* no bookstore in 2011: just video stores where college graduates would be saying, "Like, hopefully, this movie will, like, impact a fun time, like." What nostalgia I then would be feeling for the old oral culture!

Still another constant was Lori's discovery of a holly Bible in our suite, where she also found a phone in the bathroom.

"Isn't it great to call someone from in *here*!" she said.

"Yes," I replied, "but I'd still rather have toilets in telephone booths. That's what the world is waiting for."

And then the phone rang.

"Daddy, take it here!"

"Hello," I said, one foot debonairly placed on the porcelain.

"Mr. Schoenstein, this is Dottie Gold of the *Plain Dealer*. Your book is adorable."

"Thanks," I said, wondering if she wanted to see snapshots of my other books.

"I'd like to do an item about you and Lori in my column."

"The book column?"

"No, society. How do you like Cleveland?"

Suddenly, as I stood in that bathroom, trying to think of kind words for Cleveland, I could hear the musical plumber of Minneapolis starting to play and I thought:

A writer should not be doing this. A writer should not be plugging his book in a Midwestern toilet and hoping a society columnist will mention it between the horse show and the arthritis ball. This is giving new meaning to meaningless. A writer should write his book and then let the book speak for itself. And if the book has laryngitis, then, in the words of Emerson, that is too fucking bad.

However, in spite of this moment of truth, I found myself telling Dottie that *Diamonds for Lori and Me* was selling well; and, after this fanciful conversation, I spoke to Lori about tomorrow's schedule: we had a live local television show at six A.M., two live local radio shows, and visits to bookstores to prepare them for the impact of all this publicity.

"I want you to just be yourself and have fun on these shows," I told her.

"Do we have to get up at six *o'clock?*" she said. "*That's* not so much fun."

"No, not six: we have to get up at five; the show's at six. But remember, very few kids ever get a chance to go on TV with their dads."

"Daddy, who watches TV at six in the morning?"

It was a question to stand beside *Why is the sky blue?* and *Where do elephants go to die?* I decided not to answer it at once, or even that day, for I suspected that dawn TV in Cleveland might have been the equivalent of plugging my book on the television screens of a bank.

By now, I was feeling so depressed by what had to be done to sell a book, a technique I still didn't know, that I needed fresh air.

"Hey, you want to see if Cleveland has any bubble gum?" I said.

"With baseball cards," she replied.

"Absolutely. Let's get out of this dump."

And so, Lori and I went out to the city, while I tried to forget that in a few hours, I would be appearing on closed-circuit TV. As we started down Euclid Avenue, a soft evening breeze was coming from the lake and Lori let her hand fall into mine. I wanted to walk like this forever, for this was the last summer that my last daughter would be a little girl: I would soon be left alone in childhood. And now in my head I was hearing a line from a song that Lori loved: *O how I wish tomorrow would never come*, a line that didn't refer to an interviewer who would be saying, "Tell me, Lori, do you really think that diamonds are a girl's best friend?"

After we had walked for almost a block in silence, perhaps the longest silence in our gabby history, I suddenly said, "You know what our TV spots need? For you to *sing*."

"You think I *could*?" she said.

"Well, I'll have to spend most of *my* time giving the name of the book, no matter what the guy asks me; but *you* . . . with that great voice . . ."

"Right! Instead of those corny questions about why I love baseball and how it feels to be a girl, I could sing the one we made up last night:

> *Now run along home*
> *And jump into bed.*
> *Close your eyes*
> *And unscrew your head.*"

"Yes, one of our better ones, though it might not fit the interview. Of course, the questions usually don't fit the interview either, but you *should* sing something about baseball."

"If he asks me to sing 'Take Me Out to the Ball Game,' I'll throw up."

"Instead of that, just say the name of the book."

At five o'clock the following morning, after getting dressed, I uneasily sat down on her bed.

"Come on, sweetie," I said. "Time to get up and help Daddy sell another three books."

"Later," said the head retreating into the covers.

"I *know* it's hard, but just think: this is when the biggest movie stars start the day."

And this was also a scene that Dickens could have used in *Oliver Twist*: a father dragging his female child out of her bed at dawn to do some tawdry business for him.

An hour later, on the set of a local talk show whose name my mind has mercifully erased, a Dickensian poignancy was still with us.

"Honey," I whispered to Lori seconds before the show began, "try to stop yawning when the red light goes on."

The host's first question, however, did little to discourage yawning or even sleep.

"So, *Lori*," he said, "how does it *feel* to be a girl who likes baseball?"

It feels like a baseball fan with ovaries, I wanted to say, but poor Lori had to fight her own way out; and she did it well, for her IQ was at least double that of the host.

Their insightful exchange, beamed to everyone exploring new books in Cleveland at 6:05 A.M., lasted just slightly longer than the Gettysburg Address. When it was over and we had been replaced by a New Age dermatologist, I took Lori to breakfast at a coffee shop, where I searched a *Plain Dealer* for the peak of my Lake Erie print campaign. Last night, Dottie Gold had said that her interview would run today, and the thought of it had

filled me with low-grade anticipation; but now I found that her column contained not a word about Lori and me: she had deemed us less newsworthy than a pair of black pajamas worn to a gallery opening. I felt angry and ridiculous: Lori should still have been in her *own* pajamas, and *I* deserved a pair from the New Jersey Neuropsychiatric Institute.

Arthur Ashe had wisely said, "All you ever can do is to play the cards you're dealt." With this thought in mind, I watched Lori finish her French toast; and then I went off to our first Cleveland radio show, ready for another pair of twos.

The moment after she had introduced us on the air, the hostess of this show, a woman about twenty-five, said, "Lori, I know you like baseball, but let's start with a change of pace."

A change of *pace*? There was no pace to *change*: I had been *trying* to generate a pace in book publicity for twenty-eight years; but until I did, the only change possible could have been an intelligent interview.

"Tell me," said the hostess, "what's your favorite rock group?"

And then, in a derailing that at least was a happier one than Amory's on *The Mike Douglas Show*, Lori began to rhapsodize about Bon-Jovi. I was glad that we could help Bon-Jovi with their Cleveland record sales. Perhaps they would be able to return the favor at one of their concerts by stomping on a copy of *Diamonds for Lori and Me*.

After a six-minute broadcast, in which the name of my book had been an interruption, Lori and I did the one thing Judy had warned us never to do: we went into a bookstore.

"Hi!" I said with heartbreaking breeziness to a clerk behind a stack of video guides. "I'm Ralph Schoenstein and I'm doing a Cleveland media blitz for my new book, *Diamonds for Lori and Me*. I'm just wondering how it's doing."

"What's that title again?" he said, and I pictured him in the mouth of a crocodile.

"*Diamonds for Lori and Me*. It's a Book-of-the-Month Club selection."

"Yes, they take so many. No, I'm afraid I don't know it."

"But copies should have been shipped to you *ahead* of these appearances," said the author who again had been shipped instead of his books. "Are you *sure* you don't have it? *Diamonds for Lori and Me.*"

"You can look in our section on fashion, but I'm pretty sure I haven't seen it come in. We could order it for you."

We could order it for you.

These will be the last words ever heard by some poor bookstore clerk before some poor writer strangles him.

Twenty-eight years after I had gone to Chicago well ahead of *The Block*, I was back in the Midwest to publicize more phantom prose.

The next day, Lori and I were in St. Louis, where we explored only candy and record stores. Her bubbles were some of the best she had blown and Bon-Jovi was selling well.

ENTR'ACTE

Humor must surprise—in my opinion, that is; many people, all of them wrong, will disagree. It seems to me that the humorist always should be ahead of his audience and not in collaboration with them. As a boy, I never laughed at Fibber McGee's weekly radio closet, for knowing what was coming never amused me: I needed a *reversal* of expectation; and as a man, I think that a weekly "Hi, I'm Larry, this is my brother Darryl, and this is my other brother Darryl" is sitcom Sominex.

When my first editor said that Americans lack a sophisticated sense of humor, I think he meant they like humor that they can predict, though he may have meant something else. Nevertheless, whatever he meant, predictability always kills it for me. Many of Art Buchwald's Paris columns were funny because they had a surprising wackiness, but in some of his Washington ones, the comic machinery is visible at the start and then you just sing along with it, a mixed metaphor I just whipped up to see if you were paying attention. You cannot sing along with machinery unless your dishwasher makes major chords.

To me, the essence of humor is *"Shut up," he explained.* It is Robert Benchley beginning a piece:

> In the exclusive set (no diphtheria cases) in which I travel . . .

At the start of these entr'actes, E. B. White said that humor died when dissected. I hope that I have done nothing more than just bleed it a bit while poking it for a few truths. I hope I've not even come near the surgical malpractice that has grown depressingly common in our time, when pedagogic stupidity has been raised to an art form. For example, at the 1989 convention of the Modern Language Association, mankind at last came to grips with the question posed by Professor Philip Auslander of the Georgia Institute of Technology:

> Is comedy an essentially conservative genre which asks us to laugh at those who are defined as being aberrant in comparison to a socially imposed norm, or is the corrosive power of laughter a potential tool for criticizing, even dismantling, the status quo?

Had I attended the Georgia Institute of Technology, I probably would have majored in refrigeration, for I like to go with a college's strength. Nevertheless, Professor Auslander, a pretty funny writer himself, has given us not just food for thought but an entire A&P. He has plumbed aesthetic philosophy that neither Mark nor Mamie Van Doren ever considered, to wit: Is Harpo Marx aberrant in comparison to a socially imposed norm when he slices up the Prime Minister's pants in the essentially conservative genre of *Duck Soup?*

Is Harpo dismantling not only the Prime Minister's crotch but the status quo as well?

And, most important, is there something corrosive we can put in Professor Auslander's lunch?

Even the busboys at the convention of the Modern Language Association could have said with certainty that humor can be many surprising things; and I did not need Professor Auslander's transcendental dumbness to make me aware once again of the danger of sending the surprise to the clinic. For example, one day in 1988, I picked up a high school textbook called *Patterns of Language* and happily found a piece of mine coupled with a piece of Thurber's in the section teaching humor. Above the pieces were these lines:

> Humor is seeing or telling the amusing or comic side of a situation. Some situations are funny. Others are cleverly funny. Some are both funny and clever. Read the two selections that follow. To which category would you assign the selection by James Thurber? To which would you assign the selection by Ralph Schoenstein?

For the next few days, I brooded about my category, and I seemed to be flunking the course. The book had no answer to the question, Thurber was dead, and I couldn't figure out if I was cleverly funny, comically clever, comically funny, or post-Reformation wry.

At last, I managed to shake the brooding; but just a month later, I was sent a college anthology called *Style*, in which a piece of mine was followed by such questions as:

6) What is the purpose of Schoenstein's last paragraph?

Once more into the analytical breech, I tried to find the answer; and, at last, I did:

What is the purpose of my last paragraph? *It gives the piece an end.*

Epilogue

~

A Ghost for Guinness

I n the fall of 1985, after reading *Yes, My Darling Daughters*, Bill Cosby asked me to turn some of his routines about being a father into a book. Although I had written only for my own voice since my retirement as H. Allen Smith, Bill Cosby's voice had humor that touched universals; and now it was also touching the particulars of my five college loans. With the muse of Internal Revenue seizure singing softly to me, I spent three months expanding the monologues into *Fatherhood*, which became one of the biggest nonfiction best-sellers since Plato led the list. In just one city in just one week in the summer of 1986, this book not bearing my name sold more copies than the sales of all the books I had written.

Standing before a mountain of *Fatherhood* in Waldenbooks one morning, I savored the crowning absurdity of my career: although this book had enabled me to rise from debt, its publication also was the very giantism that was killing my own books. Almost laughing out loud at the thought of this unique suicide, I remembered a line by my coach, Albert Camus:

A man who has become conscious of the absurd is forever bound to it.

And now, as an anonymous entry in the *Guinness Book of World Records*, I was bound to it by Krazy Glue.

I have never been bound, however, to any literary movement or clique: I have always typed to a different drummer, one who still plays with Spike Jones; and I am writing for the endangered species that knows Spike Jones is not a guard with the Knicks. Although I have written for *The New Yorker*, *The New York Times*, *New York*, *Newsday*, and *The Village Voice*, I have never been part of a smart crowd or an in group and I have never made professional progress in an Easthampton softball game, perhaps because I play my softball behind an A&P. As Little, Brown knew, I have always fallen between pigeonholes, like some misdirected crumb. As Fred Astaire sang, I have always gone my way by myself, an itinerary that is lonely but still the best one a writer can follow. Not the most profitable or the most comfortable or the most sensible: just the best. My own books have not sold like Bill Cosby's or Laotian liquid diets, but I have seen myself in one anthology beside Mark Twain and in another beside my first literary hero, the man whose microscope revealed his own eyeball, James Thurber.

I am still an optimist, even though there are more reasons than publishing giantism to despair. I am writing in a time when a college freshman I know told me he is not taking a Western Civilization class because he is "not interested in China and Japan." I am writing in a time when garbage is being called "post-consumer secondary materials" and a death under anesthesia "a substantive negative outcome." I am writing in a time of Professor Auslander's dismantled status quo, and a Northeastern professor's appreciation of Emily Dickinson's winged vulva, and the students of a Seattle professor thinking that *The Great Gatsby* was a magician, Jefferson Davis played with the Jefferson Airplane, and Heinrich Himmler invented the Heimlich maneuver.

I am writing in the Renaissance of stupidity, when I some-times fear that proper grammar will make me sound stilted be-cause almost everyone says "*less* cases of scurvy" and "Tell Schoenstein less and less people give a damn about fewer and less"; and because even fewer of those give a damn about using "none is" instead of "none are"; and because "if I were" jars the ears of people who think the subjunctive case was one of Nero Wolfe's—no, make that one of Mike Hammer's; Nero Wolfe, as everyone knows, was the last Hebrew emperor of Rome.

I am writing in a time when more than three hundred thou-sand copies of a book called *Jimmy Stewart and His Poems* have been sold, poems that show us what Shelley might have done had he lived in west Los Angeles:

> *I'm a movie camera,*
> *Instamatic is my name.*
> *I'm Eastman's latest model.*
> *Super 8's my claim to fame.*
> *I was on a shelf in Westwood*
> *When an actor purchased me*
> *And took me home to 918 in Hills the Beverly.*

I was so moved by this flight by the Bard of the Hills the Beverly that I briefly left prose to write some verse of my own:

> *I'm a manual typewriter,*
> *Smith-Corona's my name—nifty!*
> *I'm the latest model*
> *If you've been dead since nineteen-fifty.*
> *I was in a recycling plant*
> *When Schoenstein came into view*
> *And took me home to Princeton in Jersey the New.*

In spite of this remarkable Renaissance, and in spite of all the loneliness, struggle, and absurdity of my career, there still is nothing I would rather have been than a writer: not even a symphony conductor or a center fielder or the owner of the nicest little business, for I have loved the delightfully futile business of trying to make life funny and lasting and clear; I have loved the happy delusion that I am doing something about awful randomness and rampaging time; I even have loved spending an entire day seeking the buried treasure of one right word. And, most of all, I have loved capturing the eternal good moments as I captured this one for *Newsday* in May of 1986:

HERE COMES THE BRIDE, COURAGEOUSLY

My firstborn daughter was married last night. On a warm spring evening in Philadelphia, I watched Jill and a splendid young man named Loren exchange vows and I took a break from being scared. Outside the wedding hall in Rittenhouse Square, a non-radioactive breeze rustled the trees, while inside a rabbi named Susan spoke of the union of two people in marriage as part of a universal force. How good it was to hear about a universal force that wasn't carrying roentgens, AIDS, or dynamite disguised as Snoopy dolls.

As Susan spoke of the glory of marriage, I was struck by what a lovely act of courage a wedding has become. While Khadafy burns and Kiev cooks and teenage lads go sallying forth to new capricious kills, here comes the bride courageously, marching for Donna Reed. Susan said that heaven smiles on a couple like this and for a while I forgot that heaven also weeps acid rain. She said that marriage was part of the natural order of things and gone from my mind was Ring Lardner's thought that in the natural order of things all life was eight-to-five against.

Jill had been a baby in a time before I was worried that milk might glow even more than I did from looking at her, before people in subways were trying to guess which passengers would be stabbing them, before the national pastime became paranoia. What were the odds for Jill and

Loren on this wedding day? Would Lardner have said that they were trying to make a hard eight?

"Marriage is a gratifying and intoxicating thing," Susan was saying.

As I was transported by this wedding's old-fashioned high, as Susan talked about loving each other through good times and bad, I thought of how I had protected Jill when she was small. I had protected her against the terrors of traffic, storm, and free lance writing; but now far greater terrors had become life's daily routine, and I picked up the morning paper as if holding the obituary of the world. A writer named Paul Bowles had said that everything gets worse; but as I looked at this young woman, as happy and even more beautiful now than when I had pushed her swing almost over the bar, I knew he was wrong.

". . . by the Commonwealth of Pennsylvania, I pronounce you man and wife."

Brave things have been begun in Philadelphia, I thought, as my gambler in white and her husband embraced.

The rewards of capturing life at its best, if only just for the people I love, would be enough for me. There are, however, also the rewards of hearing from strangers about my work: like a letter from Bart Giamatti calling *Diamonds for Lori and Me* "graceful, touching, and true," or a long distance call from a woman who said, "Mr. Schoenstein, I just want you to know how much I enjoyed *Every Day Is Sunday*. And it was so lucky the way I got it 'cause I hadn't gone into the Five-and-Ten for a book; I needed a mop."

"Thanks for taking the trouble to tell me that," I said.

"Have you written any *other* books?"

"Yes, more than a dozen."

"Can I find them anywhere?"

"Well, once in a while they're in bookstores, but you often

can find them in Penn Station—on that big table just outside the OTB."

"I usually use Grand Central."

"You know, I did write one bestseller you may have heard of: *The I-Hate-Preppies Handbook.*"

"*The I-Hate*-what?"

"*Preppies Handbook.* But you won't find it in Grand Central. I'm part of the Jersey Transit School."

Not long after this moving call, I happened to be strolling through Princeton's Acme and suddenly saw a big table with recently published books piled up in a jumble, a little waste dump of writers' hopes. I was about to turn away, as I always do from accidents, when I saw *Citizen Paul.* I felt as if I had found one of my children living in a bus terminal.

Picking up the book, and trying to make it look different from a can of tuna, I asked a clerk, "How much for this?"

"All of 'em are ninety-nine cents," he said.

I had dipped under a dollar, which I had always felt should have been the floor figure for my hardcover work. What was next? Was Acme the nadir? No, for an American writer in the late twentieth century, every nadir is a diving board.

Again and again as I write, no matter how much I enjoy the result, my mind cannot help returning to the question, *Who cares?* In reply, I like to think that my work will always have at least the one value that Mark Van Doren held precious when he said:

> *Wit is the only wall*
> *Between us and the dark.*

And so, once more, I sit down at my desk, move aside the latest pictures of my daughters, and try to lay another brick, probably for a wall at Woolworth's. Defeating time and chaos is, of course, the leading lost cause; but I have always had a weakness for challenges.